Still Waters

Masonic Meditations on the Book of Psalms
Volume I

Jonti Marks

First published in 2018
by
Jonti Marks

ISBN 978-0-9931127-8-2

jonti.marks@gmail.com
www.jontimarks.com

For Paddy and Val,
whose love and strength inspire us.

And for Jo,
whose love and strength inspire me.

Introduction.

This book is not in any way meant to be an explanation of the Psalms, nor does it mean to suggest that the Psalms contain any kind of secret or hidden significance for Freemasons. It is merely what it claims to be: a book of thoughts or meditations relating to Freemasonry inspired by the Psalms. It considers each Psalm in turn and uses it as a 'jumping off point' for further contemplation.

Sometimes the meditations are sparked by a word or phrase contained in the Psalm and, as such, do not necessarily relate directly to what might be considered its 'proper' meaning. Sometimes the meditation is inspired by the meaning of the Psalm and considers aspects and implications of that meaning within the context of Masonic teachings, practice and philosophy.

For a variety of aesthetic, practical and personal reasons, many of the Psalms in this book have been abridged. I make no apologies for this, I simply encourage you read the full version if you so desire. I have referred to the Deity using the pronoun 'He.' No apologies here, either - just convention.

The meditations are completely personal in so far as they are one person's thoughts, captured in one particular moment in time. It is hoped, though, that they may inspire others to consider Masonic practice more deeply and that they might become, themselves, jumping off points for further contemplation and study.

The thing about the Psalms is that they are so intensely human. Every emotion may be found here from the unutterable joy of feeling completely at one with creation to the darkest despair of abandonment and loss. Fear, uncertainty, self-doubt, loneliness, hopelessness - they are all here. Even hatred and a burning desire for vengeance and retribution. Then there is unbounded happiness and security; certainty, gratitude, the inexpressible joy of closeness to God. Whover wrote these beautiful, lyrical and sometimes dark and wrathful poems certainly knew what it was to feel and therefore knew what it was to be human.

Yet, even in the darkest moments, the writers' faith shines through. Even when they feel most abandoned, they are somehow able to glimpse that spark of divine light that, we know, will be enough to lift them out of the pit of despair into which they have fallen.

If they can do it, so can we. And here, I think, is the great attraction of these Psalms for Freemasons - and, indeed, for anyone of faith: we see clearly that even faith can falter; that even with faith, we can falter, and yet, always, if we look for it, there is enough light to bring us out of the darkness.

The Book of Psalms has been a source of inspiration to countless people for thousands of years. I hope that this little book will reacquaint you with the beauty of their language and their message and that the accompanying meditations might serve as catalysts to your own meditations and the deepening of your love and understanding of Freemasonry and of life itself.

JAM
May 2018

Psalm 1

Blessed is the man that walketh not in the counsel of the ungodly, nor standeth in the way of sinners, nor sitteth in the seat of the scornful.
2 But his delight is in the law of the LORD; and in his law doth he meditate day and night.
3 And he shall be like a tree planted by the rivers of water, that bringeth forth his fruit in his season; his leaf also shall not wither; and whatsoever he doeth shall prosper.
4 The ungodly are not so: but are like the chaff which the wind driveth away.
5 Therefore the ungodly shall not stand in the judgment, nor sinners in the congregation of the righteous.
6 For the LORD knoweth the way of the righteous: but the way of the ungodly shall perish.

Meditation 1

When we commit ourselves to the path of Freemasonry, we are, in fact, committing to a lifelong journey that will inevitably lead us towards goodness and Godliness.

Whatever the details of our particular belief-system, whatever religious or spiritual path we follow, Freemasonry enhances and decorates our faith. It is a rich and beautiful cloak that we wear over our daily practice to protect and keep it strong. Like a fine coat worn over our best clothes to protect against heavy weather, Freemasonry adds without ever taking away.

And, in putting on that protective cloak, we turn away from behaviours and thoughts that keep us tied to our earth-bound fellows and we turn our face to the long uphill path that leads to Truth and Light and Love.

Psalm 2

Why do the heathen rage, and the people imagine a vain thing?
The kings of the earth set themselves, and the rulers take counsel together, against the LORD, and against his anointed, saying,
3 Let us break their bands asunder, and cast away their cords from us.
4 He that sitteth in the heavens shall laugh: the Lord shall have them in derision.
5 Then shall he speak unto them in his wrath, and vex them in his sore displeasure.
6 Yet have I set my king upon my holy hill of Zion.
7 I will declare the decree: the LORD hath said unto me, Thou art my Son; this day have I begotten thee.
8 Ask of me, and I shall give thee the heathen for thine inheritance, and the uttermost parts of the earth for thy possession.
9 Thou shalt break them with a rod of iron; thou shalt dash them in pieces like a potter's vessel.
10 Be wise now therefore, O ye kings: be instructed, ye judges of the earth.
11 Serve the LORD with fear, and rejoice with trembling.
12 Kiss the Son, lest he be angry, and ye perish from the way, when his wrath is kindled but a little. Blessed are all they that put their trust in him.

Meditation 2

When we first set our feet on the Masonic path we can find ourselves in a lonely place. In many cases we are creating a divide, not only between ourselves and the 'outside' world, but we are also drawing a line in our own lives between what has gone before and what will come after. We have reached a point where we are ready to take responsibility for our own development as human beings – moral and spiritual – and reject the materialistic consumerism that threatens to destroy us all.

When we chart a course against the prevailing winds of the world, we encounter rough seas and many storms. Anger, hatred, mistrust – these have plagued Freemasons throughout their history and on many levels, both visible and invisible and they may raise their ugly heads to plague us even now.

But let us not worry. We know that a world of open-hearted support lies before us. The promise of universal brotherhood becomes stronger and more real with every step we take and we know, deep down, that our strength is founded on something lasting and infinitely reliable.

Psalm 3

LORD, how are they increased that trouble me! many are they that rise up against me.
2 Many there be which say of my soul, There is no help for him in God. Selah.
3 But thou, O LORD, art a shield for me; my glory, and the lifter up of mine head.
4 I cried unto the LORD with my voice, and he heard me out of his holy hill. Selah.
5 I laid me down and slept; I awaked; for the LORD sustained me.
6 I will not be afraid of ten thousands of people, that have set themselves against me round about.
7 Arise, O LORD; save me, O my God: for thou hast smitten all mine enemies upon the cheek bone; thou hast broken the teeth of the ungodly.
8 Salvation belongeth unto the LORD: thy blessing is upon thy people. Selah.

Meditation 3

The troubles of the world can seem so overpowering, so overwhelming, that we wonder how we can raise ourselves out of the pitfalls into which we so often stumble. Finances, health, relationships, work – all of these things can go wrong at any time and leave us feeling alone, abandoned and lost.

As Freemasons, we aim to practise equanimity in adversity, knowing that we are held and supported, not only by our Brotherhood, but also by our firm faith. The willingness to surrender our troubles to a Higher Power and thus to free ourselves from their hold over us is one of the greatest gifts of faith. This world is full of darkness but we know that it is also full of light. It is a wise person who can accept both joy and sorrow with a degree of acceptance and calm, knowing that, in time, all things pass, all things arise and fall away again, and only that which is true and real will last.

Psalm 4

Hear me when I call, O God of my righteousness: thou hast enlarged me when I was in distress; have mercy upon me, and hear my prayer.
2 O ye sons of men, how long will ye turn my glory into shame? how long will ye love vanity, and seek after leasing? Selah.
3 But know that the LORD hath set apart him that is godly for himself: the LORD will hear when I call unto him.
4 Stand in awe, and sin not: commune with your own heart upon your bed, and be still. Selah.
5 Offer the sacrifices of righteousness, and put your trust in the LORD.
6 There be many that say, Who will shew us any good? LORD, lift thou up the light of thy countenance upon us.
7 Thou hast put gladness in my heart, more than in the time that their corn and their wine increased.
8 I will both lay me down in peace, and sleep: for thou, LORD, only makest me dwell in safety.

Meditation 4

As Freemasons, we have tried and trusted supports to turn to when things are hard. The practical and unquestioning support of our Brethren and the rock of our faith in God both provide us with solace, comfort, help and guidance when we need it. But it is important that we do not forget to look to our own hearts to find solutions to our problems, too. If we are completely honest with ourselves – as honest as we aim to be with others – we must acknowledge that some of the responsibility for own our suffering lies with ourselves. Whether it is something we have caused to happen through our own acts of commission or omission, or merely a negative attitude to what has befallen us beyond our control, there is no doubt that we have within ourselves most of the cures for our own ills.

So, while it is vital that we learn to trust our Brothers and have faith in our God, it is also important that we look within and learn to trust ourselves.

Psalm 5

Give ear to my words, O LORD, consider my meditation. Hearken unto the voice of my cry, my King, and my God: for unto thee will I pray.
3 My voice shalt thou hear in the morning, O LORD; in the morning will I direct my prayer unto thee, and will look up.
4 For thou art not a God that hath pleasure in wickedness: neither shall evil dwell with thee.
5 The foolish shall not stand in thy sight: thou hatest all workers of iniquity.
6 Thou shalt destroy them that speak leasing: the LORD will abhor the bloody and deceitful man.
7 But as for me, I will come into thy house in the multitude of thy mercy: and in thy fear will I worship toward thy holy temple.
8 Lead me, O LORD, in thy righteousness because of mine enemies; make thy way straight before my face.
9 For there is no faithfulness in their mouth; their inward part is very wickedness; their throat is an open sepulchre; they flatter with their tongue.
10 Destroy thou them, O God; let them fall by their own counsels; cast them out in the multitude of their transgressions; for they have rebelled against thee.
11 But let all those that put their trust in thee rejoice: let them ever shout for joy, because thou defendest them: let them also that love thy name be joyful in thee.

12 For thou, LORD, wilt bless the righteous; with favour wilt thou compass him as with a shield.

Meditation 5

To live every day - ideally every moment - in conscious awareness of our relationship to our Creator; to temper our every waking thought with the remembrance of our own frailty and our ultimate mortality, these are foundation stones upon which a life of meaning and worth may be built.

It is not until we fully accept the reality of our own death that we will fully begin to live: this is one of the greatest lessons of the 3rd Degree. And while the idea of our own mortality is frightening to fully contemplate, we have, as ever, our faith to hold us up. The 'promise of futurity' mentioned in our ritual allows us to rest secure in the knowledge that, although that future might be veiled from us, it is there and we trust that we will be kept from harm. Freemasonry offers us the opportunity to be good, to be 'righteous' and we believe unhesitatingly that righteousness will be rewarded.

That certainty, that unwavering faith, is our shield.

Psalm 6

O LORD, rebuke me not in thine anger, neither chasten me in thy hot displeasure.
2 Have mercy upon me, O LORD; for I am weak: O LORD, heal me; for my bones are vexed.
3 My soul is also sore vexed: but thou, O LORD, how long?
4 Return, O LORD, deliver my soul: oh save me for thy mercies' sake.
5 For in death there is no remembrance of thee: in the grave who shall give thee thanks?
6 I am weary with my groaning; all the night make I my bed to swim; I water my couch with my tears.
7 Mine eye is consumed because of grief; it waxeth old because of all mine enemies.
8 Depart from me, all ye workers of iniquity; for the LORD hath heard the voice of my weeping.
9 The LORD hath heard my supplication; the LORD will receive my prayer.
10 Let all mine enemies be ashamed and sore vexed: let them return and be ashamed suddenly.

Meditation 6

None of us is perfect and we all have regrets in life: things we did, things we didn't do; things we said or didn't say; opportunities and connections missed and squandered. Worst of all are those moments when we know what the right thing to do is, but, often through fear, we fail to do it. In those moments we can feel such a separation from the centre of ourselves, such a distance from God, that we feel crushed, abandoned and lost. As Freemasons we strive always to be the best we can be in every moment and we are sustained and supported in this by our faith. But we are also encouraged by a system that acknowledges that we are human and that sometimes we do not live up to the high standards to which we aspire. Life is short and the silent grave awaits us all. In this certain knowledge we must learn to trust that we will be held up and comforted and that, in the end, all will be well.

Psalm 7 (abridged)

O LORD my God, in thee do I put my trust: save me from all them that persecute me, and deliver me:
8 The LORD shall judge the people: judge me, O LORD, according to my righteousness, and according to mine integrity that is in me.
9 Oh let the wickedness of the wicked come to an end; but establish the just: for the righteous God trieth the hearts and reins.
10 My defence is of God, which saveth the upright in heart.
11 God judgeth the righteous, and God is angry with the wicked every day.
12 If he turn not, he will whet his sword; he hath bent his bow, and made it ready.
13 He hath also prepared for him the instruments of death; he ordaineth his arrows against the persecutors.
14 Behold, he travaileth with iniquity, and hath conceived mischief, and brought forth falsehood.
15 He made a pit, and digged it, and is fallen into the ditch which he made.
16 His mischief shall return upon his own head, and his violent dealing shall come down upon his own pate.
17 I will praise the LORD according to his righteousness: and will sing praise to the name of the LORD most high.

Meditation 7

While the idea that we should 'let go and let God' is one that is central to our sense of ourselves as Freemasons, we also understand ourselves to be co-creators of that perfect world of peace and harmony that is our goal and our dream. Our obligation and our duty in the world is to act at all times in the consciousness of our belief in the brotherhood and sisterhood of all of humanity; to bring harmony where there is strife; to relieve suffering; to comfort those who are in distress; to do all we can to actualize the philosophy to which we have subscribed.

And while we are committed to action, we also recognise that, without our belief in God, our actions have no meaning and no authority. We must act, of course we must, but we must also understand that, through us, God acts. Through us, God is known.

Freemasons are committed to a better world and a better life for all, regardless of race, sex, sexuality, belief or any other potentially dividing factors. Freemasons understand that we are all the beloved children of one God and so we work only for the common good. We do not presume to judge or punish, only to praise and encourage.

All the rest, we can leave to Providence.

Psalm 8

O LORD our Lord, how excellent is thy name in all the earth! who hast set thy glory above the heavens.
2 Out of the mouth of babes and sucklings hast thou ordained strength because of thine enemies, that thou mightest still the enemy and the avenger.
3 When I consider thy heavens, the work of thy fingers, the moon and the stars, which thou hast ordained;
4 What is man, that thou art mindful of him? and the son of man, that thou visitest him?
5 For thou hast made him a little lower than the angels, and hast crowned him with glory and honour.
6 Thou madest him to have dominion over the works of thy hands; thou hast put all things under his feet:
7 All sheep and oxen, yea, and the beasts of the field;
8 The fowl of the air, and the fish of the sea, and whatsoever passeth through the paths of the seas.
9 O LORD our Lord, how excellent is thy name in all the earth!

Meditation 8

There are times when we need to stop what we are doing; when we must step back from our constant striving, our busy-ness and look around us. The world is beautiful and full of wonder and it is vital for our continued well-being, inner peace and mental health that we take the time to appreciate it. Never underestimate the benefit of a walk in the park or a day in the country. If that's not possible, just look out of the window or up at the sky. Contemplate, just for a moment the expanse of the heavens and the complexity and variety of life here on earth. How can we not be filled with a sense of awe and wonder at this daily miracle that we call life?

And consider us - human beings - our ability to choose between right and wrong, our ability to be conscious of our thoughts, our gift of free will. How wondrous we are and what a responsibility we carry!

In these moments of realisation are to be found the keys to our true relationship to each other and to our Creator. Part of our duty as Freemasons is to look for opportunities to experience those moments and to share them, as far as is possible, with others.

Psalm 9 (abridged)

I will praise thee, O LORD, with my whole heart; I will shew forth all thy marvellous works.
2 I will be glad and rejoice in thee: I will sing praise to thy name, O thou most High.
4 For thou hast maintained my right and my cause; thou satest in the throne judging right.
5 Thou hast rebuked the heathen, thou hast destroyed the wicked, thou hast put out their name for ever and ever.
7 But the LORD shall endure for ever: he hath prepared his throne for judgment.
8 And he shall judge the world in righteousness, he shall minister judgment to the people in uprightness.
9 The LORD also will be a refuge for the oppressed, a refuge in times of trouble.
10 And they that know thy name will put their trust in thee: for thou, LORD, hast not forsaken them that seek thee.
11 Sing praises to the LORD, which dwelleth in Zion: declare among the people his doings.
15 The heathen are sunk down in the pit that they made: in the net which they hid is their own foot taken.
16 The LORD is known by the judgment which he executeth: the wicked is snared in the work of his own hands.
18 For the needy shall not always be forgotten: the expectation of the poor shall not perish for ever.

19 Arise, O LORD; let not man prevail: let the heathen be judged in thy sight.
20 Put them in fear, O LORD: that the nations may know themselves to be but men. Selah.

Meditation 9

One of our most important responsibilities as Freemasons has nothing - or very little - to do with what goes on within our Lodges. While our ceremonies and the times we spend together are important in so far as they inspire and strengthen us, they are of little value if we don't carry what we learn into our everyday lives. The truth of God's love for all, the truth that we are all God's children, the understanding that we are all part of one life, united and indivisible: that's what we are called upon to demonstrate.
It doesn't mean that we have to talk about it; it doesn't mean we have to impose our understanding of the world on others - we can trust God to do that when the time is right - it simply means that we must act in the light of what we know. Freemasons are always there to help and support; to offer a kind word and a helping hand because we know that it is through our response to the suffering and distress of others that the validity of our path is judged.
When we act from the highest that is within us, we cannot help but shine a light on our Creator's 'marvellous works.'

Psalm 10 (abridged)

Why standest thou afar off, O LORD? why hidest thou thyself in times of trouble?
2 The wicked in his pride doth persecute the poor:
4 The wicked, through the pride of his countenance, will not seek after God: God is not in all his thoughts.
5 His ways are always grievous; thy judgments are far above out of his sight: as for all his enemies, he puffeth at them.
6 He hath said in his heart, I shall not be moved: for I shall never be in adversity.
7 His mouth is full of cursing and deceit and fraud: under his tongue is mischief and vanity.
9 He lieth in wait secretly as a lion in his den: he lieth in wait to catch the poor: he doth catch the poor, when he draweth him into his net.
11 He hath said in his heart, God hath forgotten: he hideth his face; he will never see it.
12 Arise, O LORD; O God, lift up thine hand: forget not the humble.
13 Wherefore doth the wicked contemn God? he hath said in his heart, Thou wilt not require it.
14 Thou hast seen it; for thou beholdest mischief and spite, to requite it with thy hand: the poor committeth himself unto thee; thou art the helper of the fatherless.
16 The LORD is King for ever and ever: the heathen are perished out of his land.

17 LORD, thou hast heard the desire of the humble: thou wilt prepare their heart, thou wilt cause thine ear to hear:
18 To judge the fatherless and the oppressed, that the man of the earth may no more oppress.

Meditation 10

It's hard to understand sometimes quite how the world works. When we are committed to a path of service, founded on a firm belief in the concept of Universal Brotherhood, it can be difficult to see good people struggling and suffering while others, who seem to live only for themselves, prosper. The question of how we, as Freemasons, confront such injustice in the world is an important one. We are enjoined to refrain from discussing both politics and religion in our meetings, and yet both of these things have a profound bearing on the problem. We are not revolutionaries, that much is clear, but neither are we silent and indifferent bystanders to injustice, poverty and suffering. Our response – a beautifully Masonic one – must be to relieve suffering where we see it, irrespective of the sufferer's race or creed or whatever. We stand firm for the values we believe in – by exemplifying them in all our words and deeds – and thus we anticipate and subvert any revolutionary impulses by acting with love and kindness to all those who suffer. At the same time we encourage responsibility and selflessness in those who have power to make changes.
Perhaps we are revolutionaries after all!

Psalm 11

In the LORD put I my trust: how say ye to my soul, Flee as a bird to your mountain?
2 For, lo, the wicked bend their bow, they make ready their arrow upon the string, that they may privily shoot at the upright in heart.
3 If the foundations be destroyed, what can the righteous do?
4 The LORD is in his holy temple, the LORD'S throne is in heaven: his eyes behold, his eyelids try, the children of men.
5 The LORD trieth the righteous: but the wicked and him that loveth violence his soul hateth.
6 Upon the wicked he shall rain snares, fire and brimstone, and an horrible tempest: this shall be the portion of their cup.
7 For the righteous LORD loveth righteousness; his countenance doth behold the upright.

Meditation 11

All of life evolves and moves forward. This is especially true when it comes to the development of human consciousness and the maturity of our faith. The slow dawning of understand from animism to polytheism to monotheism and the idea of unity is one such development. But we can go further and, as Freemasons, we are committed to doing so. When we place God outside of ourselves, on a throne, in Heaven, we look to Him to right our wrongs, to fight our battles and to see that justice is done; we relate to Him as children: needy and dependent.

When we place God in our hearts, however, we begin to step into our true relationship with Him, as co-creators of a better world – a world where we see Him in the hearts of all our Brothers and Sisters. We begin to take responsibility for our own world. We begin to stand up against injustice and look to remedy it from the depths of our understanding of the true nature of brotherly love.

The Temple that we Freemasons are building is not a physical one. The Temple of heaven exists, we believe that and we understand it each in our own way; but the Temple we seek to build in our daily lives is the one in our hearts, and we must make it fit to contain the eternal presence of the Most High.

Psalm 12

Help, LORD; for the godly man ceaseth; for the faithful fail from among the children of men.
2 They speak vanity every one with his neighbour: with flattering lips and with a double heart do they speak.
3 The LORD shall cut off all flattering lips, and the tongue that speaketh proud things:
4 Who have said, With our tongue will we prevail; our lips are our own: who is lord over us?
5 For the oppression of the poor, for the sighing of the needy, now will I arise, saith the LORD; I will set him in safety from him that puffeth at him.
6 The words of the LORD are pure words: as silver tried in a furnace of earth, purified seven times.
7 Thou shalt keep them, O LORD, thou shalt preserve them from this generation for ever.
8 The wicked walk on every side, when the vilest men are exalted.

Meditation 12

The values that Freemasonry promotes are sometimes so at odds with the values of the world that we can feel that we are surrounded by a kind of madness. How can it be that we, who are steeped in the understanding that all of life is one life, are able to function in societies that divide brother from brother; that allow war, hunger, disease, hatred and destruction to prevail? We go to our Lodges and we glorify the concepts of equality and the brotherhood of all humanity, but beyond those Lodge walls, we are thrown into a chaos of conflict. How do we hold on to our equilibrium?

Well, we have our faith, for one thing. Masonically speaking, we know that at the core of that circle of faith there is a point of stillness from which clarity and calmness emanate. That point within the circle represents the core of ourselves, the spiritual, God-attuned reality of who and what we are. Freemasonry gives us the tools to look within ourselves to find that still centre and, with practice, we can learn to act from it, to retreat to it and to draw from it all the resources we need to cope with the vagaries and difficulties of the outside world.

Psalm 13

How long wilt thou forget me, O LORD? for ever? how long wilt thou hide thy face from me?

2 How long shall I take counsel in my soul, having sorrow in my heart daily? how long shall mine enemy be exalted over me?

3 Consider and hear me, O LORD my God: lighten mine eyes, lest I sleep the sleep of death;

4 Lest mine enemy say, I have prevailed against him; and those that trouble me rejoice when I am moved.

5 But I have trusted in thy mercy; my heart shall rejoice in thy salvation.

6 I will sing unto the LORD, because he hath dealt bountifully with me.

Meditation 13

There's no such thing as an easy ride in life. Sometimes we can look at others who appear to be so much better off than us, whether in terms of money, work, health, happiness or anything and everything else – from the house they live in to the car they drive to the quality of their relationships – and wish we had what they have. Jealousy and resentment lie in wait for us, ready to distort our world view and steal our peace of mind. If we look a little deeper, though, we find that it is all an illusion. Everybody has their troubles and disappointments; every life has worry and sadness; every life ends, ultimately, in death.

As Freemasons, we know this and try to hold ourselves steady through all the vagaries of life. We deal with ourselves and with others with compassion and understanding because, when all is said and done, we have that calm centre of faith and trust that helps us stay anchored in things that are real and true.

Psalm 14

The fool hath said in his heart, There is no God. They are corrupt, they have done abominable works, there is none that doeth good.

2 The LORD looked down from heaven upon the children of men, to see if there were any that did understand, and seek God.

3 They are all gone aside, they are all together become filthy: there is none that doeth good, no, not one.

4 Have all the workers of iniquity no knowledge? who eat up my people as they eat bread, and call not upon the LORD.

5 There were they in great fear: for God is in the generation of the righteous.

6 Ye have shamed the counsel of the poor, because the LORD is his refuge.

7 Oh that the salvation of Israel were come out of Zion! when the LORD bringeth back the captivity of his people, Jacob shall rejoice, and Israel shall be glad.

Meditation 14

Being a Freemason carries a great weight of responsibility. Once we are committed to the path and once we begin to understand where it leads, it is our duty to ourselves, our brethren and to the world at large to always act upon and live according to the precepts we profess to admire. It's no good extolling the virtues of brotherhood in Lodge if we don't go out into the world and demonstrate those virtues in our daily lives. It's pointless and hypocritical to align ourselves to the Masonic values of brotherly love, relief and truth if we don't go out into the world and hold up those values in all of our dealings with others.

To be ignorant is one thing – ignorance can be overcome through education; but to know something to be true and then not to act on it, that is worse than ignorance, that is a character fault and an act of shame from which we, as Masons, must work, in every moment of every day, to free ourselves.

Psalm 15

LORD, who shall abide in thy tabernacle? who shall dwell in thy holy hill?
2 He that walketh uprightly, and worketh righteousness, and speaketh the truth in his heart.
3 He that backbiteth not with his tongue, nor doeth evil to his neighbour, nor taketh up a reproach against his neighbour.
4 In whose eyes a vile person is contemned; but he honoureth them that fear the LORD. He that sweareth to his own hurt, and changeth not.
5 He that putteth not out his money to usury, nor taketh reward against the innocent. He that doeth these things shall never be moved.

Meditation 15

In our ritual we talk about the 'benefits' of Freemasonry but we don't always clearly define exactly what they are.

Of course, some of the benefits are obvious. We take pleasure in the sense of comradeship that is to be found in our Lodges. We enjoy being in an environment where our honesty and integrity are taken as a given. We have fun: we laugh together and enjoy the company of people whom we might not otherwise find a chance to get to know.

Some benefits are mentioned in the ritual, however; deeper and perhaps more personal. For example, there is a reference to the joy of living with a clear conscience and, in a way, the sense of inner calm and serenity that comes from knowing that we are always trying to be the best that we can be, may be seen as another way of expressing, at least figuratively, that we are living our lives ever closer to God, under His protection, in His house.

Psalm 16

Preserve me, O God: for in thee do I put my trust.
O my soul, thou hast said unto the LORD, Thou art my Lord: my goodness extendeth not to thee;
3 But to the saints that are in the earth, and to the excellent, in whom is all my delight.
4 Their sorrows shall be multiplied that hasten after another god: their drink offerings of blood will I not offer, nor take up their names into my lips.
5 The LORD is the portion of mine inheritance and of my cup: thou maintainest my lot.
6 The lines are fallen unto me in pleasant places; yea, I have a goodly heritage.
7 I will bless the LORD, who hath given me counsel: my reins also instruct me in the night seasons.
8 I have set the LORD always before me: because he is at my right hand, I shall not be moved.
9 Therefore my heart is glad, and my glory rejoiceth: my flesh also shall rest in hope.
10 For thou wilt not leave my soul in hell; neither wilt thou suffer thine Holy One to see corruption.
11 Thou wilt shew me the path of life: in thy presence is fulness of joy; at thy right hand there are pleasures for evermore.

Meditation 16

Trust and patience are two of the great lessons that Freemasonry can teach us; two of the gifts that it offers, From the moment that we approach a known Brother to ask about the Order; from that moment of aloneness as we wait outside the door of the Lodge before being initiated; from that moment when we kneel in darkness – we trust. We trust ourselves and the intuitions that led us to enquire about Freemasonry and then to seek admission. We trust the people we met who put us on the path; we trust those who prepare us and who conduct us into the Lodge to receive the blessing of light.

And then we learn patience because patience is trust that things will work out in their due time. We progress slowly, passing to the second degree, being raised to the third. We begin to work in the Lodge and then to take offices, perhaps eventually being honoured with the opportunity to sit in the Master's chair.

All this can take years and then there is more beyond this, as we know. But we learn to accept, to understand that the system we are a part of is well-designed and that, as each step is presented to us, we are readied to meet it.

And as it is in Freemasonry, so it is with life.

Psalm 17 (abridged)

Hear the right, O LORD, attend unto my cry, give ear unto my prayer, that goeth not out of feigned lips.
2 Let my sentence come forth from thy presence; let thine eyes behold the things that are equal.
3 Thou hast proved mine heart; thou hast visited me in the night; thou hast tried me, and shalt find nothing; I am purposed that my mouth shall not transgress.
4 Concerning the works of men, by the word of thy lips I have kept me from the paths of the destroyer.
5 Hold up my goings in thy paths, that my footsteps slip not.
6 I have called upon thee, for thou wilt hear me, O God: incline thine ear unto me, and hear my speech.
7 Shew thy marvellous lovingkindness, O thou that savest by thy right hand them which put their trust in thee from those that rise up against them.
8 Keep me as the apple of the eye, hide me under the shadow of thy wings,
15 As for me, I will behold thy face in righteousness: I shall be satisfied, when I awake, with thy likeness.

Meditation 17

There is an assumption that when someone seeks admission into our order, they are motivated by the best of intentions. Our ritual makes it clear: we are asked if we come to solicit the privileges of Initiation as a result of "...a favourable opinion preconceived of the Institution, a general desire of knowledge, and a sincere wish to render yourself more extensively serviceable to your fellow-creatures..."

So when we first knock at the door of Freemasonry, we have already made the first steps towards the perfection of our lives. The claim that Freemasonry 'makes good men better' is not an idle one. We come already predisposed to want to learn and to serve and it is these things that open the door to us and allow us to progress on our journey.

Perhaps the greatest pitfall that awaits us is that of hubris. We know the path we are on and, while we recognise that it is not the only path, we are aware that it is a path that leads us away from and above the common condition of humanity towards the Godhead. This is why a genuine and constant humility is necessary. The moment we begin to feel ourselves to be better than others, we abandon our principles of universal brotherhood and we lose every advantage that Freemasonry gives us.

If we are to walk a righteous, path, it must be in the sure knowledge that we are able to do so only because we walk in the shadow and under the guidance and protection of God.

Psalm 18 (abridged)

I will love thee, O LORD, my strength.
The LORD is my rock, and my fortress, and my deliverer; my God, my strength, in whom I will trust;
3 I will call upon the LORD, who is worthy to be praised: so shall I be saved from mine enemies.
4 The sorrows of death compassed me, and the floods of ungodly men made me afraid.
5 The sorrows of hell compassed me about: the snares of death prevented me.
6 In my distress I called upon the LORD, and cried unto my God: he heard my voice out of his temple, and my cry came before him, even into his ears.
17 He delivered me from my strong enemy, and from them which hated me: for they were too strong for me.
19 He brought me forth also into a large place; he delivered me, because he delighted in me.
20 The LORD rewarded me according to my righteousness; according to the cleanness of my hands hath he recompensed me.
46 The LORD liveth; and blessed be my rock; and let the God of my salvation be exalted.
47 It is God that avengeth me, and subdueth the people under me.
48 He delivereth me from mine enemies: yea, thou liftest me up above those that rise up against me: thou hast

delivered me from the violent man.
49 Therefore will I give thanks unto thee, O LORD, among the heathen, and sing praises unto thy name.
50 Great deliverance giveth he to his king; and sheweth mercy to his anointed, to David, and to his seed for evermore.

Meditation 18

In some ways, it's easy to love an abstracted image of perfection and there is no doubt that when we try to imagine the Divine, we tend to create it as an idealisation of what we are. Therefore God becomes, to us, a projection of what we see as the very best in ourselves.

What's more difficult to understand and accept is that God doesn't just exist 'out there' but also, and more importantly, in every aspect of Earthly existence. And, while we know that the earth is full of beauty and that we humans are capable of the most altruistic and noble acts, some of it is pretty ugly.

For us to learn to see God equally in every human being, in every animal and plant – in every living entity – is, spiritually, a herculean task. To see Spirit move in beauty and goodness is easy enough, but to see it in squalor and degradation, in war, murder, hatred and indifference is another thing entirely.

If we are to build a house fit for the Lord with our lives, it must be large enough – our hearts must be open enough – to include everyone, not just those who appear to be 'deserving.'

When we can do this, then we can truly claim to love the Lord.

Psalm 19 (abridged)

The heavens declare the glory of God; and the firmament sheweth his handywork.
2 Day unto day uttereth speech, and night unto night sheweth knowledge.
3 There is no speech nor language, where their voice is not heard.
6 His going forth is from the end of the heaven, and his circuit unto the ends of it: and there is nothing hid from the heat thereof.
7 The law of the LORD is perfect, converting the soul: the testimony of the LORD is sure, making wise the simple.
8 The statutes of the LORD are right, rejoicing the heart: the commandment of the LORD is pure, enlightening the eyes.
9 The fear of the LORD is clean, enduring for ever: the judgments of the LORD are true and righteous altogether.
10 More to be desired are they than gold, yea, than much fine gold: sweeter also than honey and the honeycomb.
11 Moreover by them is thy servant warned: and in keeping of them there is great reward.
12 Who can understand his errors? cleanse thou me from secret faults.
13 Keep back thy servant also from presumptuous sins; let them not have dominion over me: then shall I be upright, and I shall be innocent from the great transgression.
14 Let the words of my mouth, and the meditation of my

heart, be acceptable in thy sight, O LORD, my strength, and my redeemer.

Meditation 19

As Freemasons, it must be part of our daily practice to learn to love and appreciate this beautiful world in which we live. We know – and our ritual reminds us – that the Earth is made with symmetry and order and that Wisdom, Strength and Beauty are inextricably woven into its fabric. We must also remember, though, that this life is not all that there is. To be wholly seduced by its attractions is not our purpose and we must keep in mind that greater existence which is our birthright and our source.

The teachings of Freemasonry are enough to keep us on track at all times and the support and companionship of our Brethren are enough to give us the strength to continue, even when life challenges us to the limits of our capacity to cope.

This practice, this path, this hope of futurity – these are the things of true value in the world. It is no coincidence that we are given a password whose import is 'worldly possessions' moments before we are led to a figurative death and it is only in the light of true brotherhood under God that we are raised again.

Sweeter than gold? Definitely.

Psalm 20

The LORD hear thee in the day of trouble; the name of the God of Jacob defend thee;
2 Send thee help from the sanctuary, and strengthen thee out of Zion;
3 Remember all thy offerings, and accept thy burnt sacrifice; Selah.
4 Grant thee according to thine own heart, and fulfil all thy counsel.
5 We will rejoice in thy salvation, and in the name of our God we will set up our banners: the LORD fulfil all thy petitions.
6 Now know I that the LORD saveth his anointed; he will hear him from his holy heaven with the saving strength of his right hand.
7 Some trust in chariots, and some in horses: but we will remember the name of the LORD our God.
8 They are brought down and fallen: but we are risen, and stand upright.
9 Save, LORD: let the king hear us when we call.

Meditation 20

We take so much on trust in our lives, but if we didn't we would never be able to lift ourselves out of a bottomless pit of anxiety and worry.

Who has access to our bank details? What social media platform is selling our personal preferences? What kind of person is teaching my children? Who's got their finger on the nuclear button? There are endless things to fret about and many of them are real and worthy of a certain amount of attention. The trick, though, is to only give them the amount of attention they deserve, proportional to the importance they have in our lives.

So check your on-line marketplaces and your Facebook settings. Meet your children's teachers; vote wisely in elections. Do what you can.

And then let go.

Our ritual says: "...relying on such sure support you may safely rise and follow your leader with a firm but humble confidence, for where the name of GOD is invoked, we trust no danger can ensue." Of course, this alludes to a particular moment at our Initiation, but the principle remains true in the whole circle of our lives.

Trust is a valid and effective antidote to worry as long as it is well-founded. Ours, being founded on God, is strong enough to overcome all that troubles us.

Psalm 21

The king shall joy in thy strength, O LORD; and in thy salvation how greatly shall he rejoice!
2 Thou hast given him his heart's desire, and hast not withholden the request of his lips. Selah.
3 For thou preventest him with the blessings of goodness: thou settest a crown of pure gold on his head.
4 He asked life of thee, and thou gavest it him, even length of days for ever and ever.
5 His glory is great in thy salvation: honour and majesty hast thou laid upon him.
6 For thou hast made him most blessed for ever: thou hast made him exceeding glad with thy countenance.
7 For the king trusteth in the LORD, and through the mercy of the most High he shall not be moved.
8 Thine hand shall find out all thine enemies: thy right hand shall find out those that hate thee.
9 Thou shalt make them as a fiery oven in the time of thine anger: the LORD shall swallow them up in his wrath, and the fire shall devour them.
10 Their fruit shalt thou destroy from the earth, and their seed from among the children of men.
11 For they intended evil against thee: they imagined a mischievous device, which they are not able to perform.
12 Therefore shalt thou make them turn their back, when thou shalt make ready thine arrows upon thy strings against

the face of them.
13 Be thou exalted, LORD, in thine own strength: so will we sing and praise thy power.

Meditation 21

Wisdom, strength and beauty are the three pillars which support a Freemason's Lodge. They are described as three attributes with which God is imbued and which are manifest in creation. As such, we can also understand them to be three excellences of character to which we should aspire.
The strength that we - frail creatures that we are - must learn is not necessarily about physical strength although it is certain that what physical strength we have must be put to use in service and doing good works. More importantly, though, the strength we must cultivate must be internal: strength of character; firmness of faith, an unwavering commitment to do and be our best at all times.
To live in accord with what we know to be true, this is the first step to wisdom; and if we live in wisdom and strength, surely our lives will be beautiful.

Psalm 22 (abridged)

My God, my God, why hast thou forsaken me? why art thou so far from helping me, and from the words of my roaring?
2 O my God, I cry in the daytime, but thou hearest not; and in the night season, and am not silent.
3 But thou art holy, O thou that inhabitest the praises of Israel.
4 Our fathers trusted in thee: they trusted, and thou didst deliver them.
5 They cried unto thee, and were delivered: they trusted in thee, and were not confounded.
7 All they that see me laugh me to scorn: they shoot out the lip, they shake the head, saying,
8 He trusted on the LORD that he would deliver him: let him deliver him, seeing he delighted in him.
9 But thou art he that took me out of the womb: thou didst make me hope when I was upon my mother's breasts.
10 I was cast upon thee from the womb: thou art my God from my mother's belly.
11 Be not far from me; for trouble is near; for there is none to help.
22 I will declare thy name unto my brethren: in the midst of the congregation will I praise thee.
23 Ye that fear the LORD, praise him; all ye the seed of Jacob, glorify him; and fear him, all ye the seed of Israel.

27 All the ends of the world shall remember and turn unto the LORD: and all the kindreds of the nations shall worship before thee.
28 For the kingdom is the LORD'S: and he is the governor among the nations.

Meditation 22

Freemasons live in two worlds that sometimes seem totally incompatible. On the one hand, we live and work in the world of external form. We do our duty - to ourselves, our families and our connections; we conform to social expectations and uphold the laws of our respective lands. Our lives, sometimes, are hard. We put in long hours at our workplace, we struggle to find a balance between what we must do and what we want to do. If we are lucky, the two occasionally merge but, in the daily struggle, God can seem very far away.

And yet, we also carry within us another world. A world of knowledge and deep understanding that, beyond this life there is another existence. The world is not what it appears to be and those of us lucky enough to have been given a glimpse beyond its veils, know that there is more.

When life is busy, difficult, chaotic; when we struggle and feel abandoned and alone, we need to remember what is on the other side of that veil. Stop for a moment. Breathe. Think.

God is there.

Psalm 23

The LORD is my shepherd; I shall not want.
He maketh me to lie down in green pastures: he leadeth me beside the still waters.
3 He restoreth my soul: he leadeth me in the paths of righteousness for his name's sake.
4 Yea, though I walk through the valley of the shadow of death, I will fear no evil: for thou art with me; thy rod and thy staff they comfort me.
5 Thou preparest a table before me in the presence of mine enemies: thou anointest my head with oil; my cup runneth over.
6 Surely goodness and mercy shall follow me all the days of my life: and I will dwell in the house of the LORD for ever.

Meditation 23

In the relentless busy-ness of our lives, the idea of just stopping for a moment can be terrifying. We are so used to believing that our striving is all that keeps us from ruin that we forget who we truly are and why we are really here.

Of course, we must take care of our material needs as far as we are able. We must clothe and feed ourselves and our families. There are bills to pay, mortgages to service, contingencies to plan for. But unless we take the time to focus, to find our centre, to remind ourselves of who and what we are, we run the risk of losing ourselves and succumbing to a weight of care that can overwhelm us.

It is at these times that we most need to remember that, beyond this life, another existence is possible. If we can't do it literally, then we must find time to do it metaphorically: to lie down in those green pastures; to drink of those still waters; to restore our soul.

Psalm 24

The earth is the LORD'S, and the fulness thereof; the world, and they that dwell therein.
2 For he hath founded it upon the seas, and established it upon the floods.
3 Who shall ascend into the hill of the LORD? or who shall stand in his holy place?
4 He that hath clean hands, and a pure heart; who hath not lifted up his soul unto vanity, nor sworn deceitfully.
5 He shall receive the blessing from the LORD, and righteousness from the God of his salvation.
6 This is the generation of them that seek him, that seek thy face, O Jacob. Selah.
7 Lift up your heads, O ye gates; and be ye lift up, ye everlasting doors; and the King of glory shall come in.
8 Who is this King of glory? The LORD strong and mighty, the LORD mighty in battle.
9 Lift up your heads, O ye gates; even lift them up, ye everlasting doors; and the King of glory shall come in.
10 Who is this King of glory? The LORD of hosts, he is the King of glory. Selah.

Meditation 24

The idea of ascent is a strong one in Freemasonry. In the first degree, we are told of Jacob's ladder and of how we might attain its summit. In the second degree we hear a great deal about the winding staircase and how all duly qualified brethren were able to climb it and thus reach the Middle Chamber of the Temple where they received their wages and discovered the sacred symbol. In the third degree, we are 'raised' from a figurative death to glimpse the possibilty of a new life.

In the Royal Arch, our ascent is preceded by a descent into darkness where we find the light that will allow us to be lifted up again.

The symbolism of these ascents is clear: we rise slowly from the physical to the spiritual; from the earthly plane to the heavenly; from darkness upwards to the Light.

And how do we make this great ascent?

Slowly, but surely: with clean hands and pure hearts. Our actions will bring their own rewards.

Psalm 25 (abridged)

Unto thee, O LORD, do I lift up my soul.
Lead me in thy truth, and teach me: for thou art the God of my salvation; on thee do I wait all the day.
6 Remember, O LORD, thy tender mercies and thy lovingkindnesses; for they have been ever of old.
7 Remember not the sins of my youth, nor my transgressions: according to thy mercy remember thou me for thy goodness' sake, O LORD.
8 Good and upright is the LORD: therefore will he teach sinners in the way.
9 The meek will he guide in judgment: and the meek will he teach his way.
10 All the paths of the LORD are mercy and truth unto such as keep his covenant and his testimonies.
14 The secret of the LORD is with them that fear him; and he will shew them his covenant.
15 Mine eyes are ever toward the LORD; for he shall pluck my feet out of the net.
16 Turn thee unto me, and have mercy upon me; for I am desolate and afflicted.
17 The troubles of my heart are enlarged: O bring thou me out of my distresses.
18 Look upon mine affliction and my pain; and forgive all my sins.
19 Consider mine enemies; for they are many; and they

hate me with cruel hatred.
20 O keep my soul, and deliver me: let me not be ashamed; for I put my trust in thee.
21 Let integrity and uprightness preserve me; for I wait on thee.
22 Redeem Israel, O God, out of all his troubles.

Meditation 25

One of the great things about Freemasonry is that, while it calls on us to be the best that we can be, it never asks us to be more than we can be.
None of us is perfect and all of us have made mistakes and errors of judgement which, with the gift of hindsight, we might come to regret. Guilt is a debilitating emotion that prevents us from living fully in the moment. It infects our present with the poisons of our past and means that we can never attain that ease and clarity and singlesness of character to which we aspire.
The only way to be fully free is to learn forgiveness and it is here that Freemasonry's benevolence can be seen. By assuming the best of us in the here and now, it allows us to forgive ourselves. More importantly, it also calls on us to forgive others and, in doing so it allows us to cultivate those truly Masonic virtues of truth, of mercy and of kindness.

Psalm 26

Judge me, O LORD; for I have walked in mine integrity: I have trusted also in the LORD; therefore I shall not slide.
2 Examine me, O LORD, and prove me; try my reins and my heart.
3 For thy lovingkindness is before mine eyes: and I have walked in thy truth.
4 I have not sat with vain persons, neither will I go in with dissemblers.
5 I have hated the congregation of evil doers; and will not sit with the wicked.
6 I will wash mine hands in innocency: so will I compass thine altar, O LORD:
7 That I may publish with the voice of thanksgiving, and tell of all thy wondrous works.
8 LORD, I have loved the habitation of thy house, and the place where thine honour dwelleth.
9 Gather not my soul with sinners, nor my life with bloody men:
10 In whose hands is mischief, and their right hand is full of bribes.
11 But as for me, I will walk in mine integrity: redeem me, and be merciful unto me.
12 My foot standeth in an even place: in the congregations will I bless the LORD.

Meditation 26

One of the earliest charges laid upon us as Freemasons is that each one of us should aim to be a '...good man and true...'

The idea of truth in this sense is about more than just a narrow idea of being honest in what we say - although, of course, that is a meaning that must be included. But to be a 'true' man is something more. It's about carrying with us at all times a sense of unity of purpose and of being. The words we say, the thoughts we think and the actions we perform all arise from a centre of integration wherein our personality and our deeper spiritual selves are fully aligned.

More than this, it's also about having a conscience and working to keep that conscience clear. In other words, we work constantly and in every moment to see the right in every circumstance and then to act upon that knowing. By doing this we remain, in all senses, true to ourselves, true to the moral principles of our order and true to God.

Psalm 27 (abridged)

The LORD is my light and my salvation; whom shall I fear? the LORD is the strength of my life; of whom shall I be afraid?
4 One thing have I desired of the LORD, that will I seek after; that I may dwell in the house of the LORD all the days of my life, to behold the beauty of the LORD, and to enquire in his temple.
5 For in the time of trouble he shall hide me in his pavilion: in the secret of his tabernacle shall he hide me; he shall set me up upon a rock.
7 Hear, O LORD, when I cry with my voice: have mercy also upon me, and answer me.
8 When thou saidst, Seek ye my face; my heart said unto thee, Thy face, LORD, will I seek.
9 Hide not thy face far from me; put not thy servant away in anger: thou hast been my help; leave me not, neither forsake me, O God of my salvation.
10 When my father and my mother forsake me, then the LORD will take me up.
11 Teach me thy way, O LORD, and lead me in a plain path, because of mine enemies.
14 Wait on the LORD: be of good courage, and he shall strengthen thine heart: wait, I say, on the LORD.

Meditation 27

Fear is a great force in all of our lives and, conscious or not, many of our decisions are taken in its shadow. We are in its grip from our earliest years, from the great fear of annihilation to the small fears of insecurity and doing the wrong thing.

Eventually fear becomes so integrated into who we are that we stop recognising it as such and we find ourselves conforming to rules and mores that, quite often, don't actually exist except in the confines of our own heads. Fear can destabilise us. It can take us away from who we are and prevent us becoming all that we might be. It can inhibit our joy, block our creativity, stunt our growth and stifle our ability to give and receive love.

"Fear of the Lord is the beginning of wisdom" and it may be that, really, the only thing we need to fear is the consequence of not living up to our full potential as co-creators of what Charles Eisenstein calls 'the beautiful world we know is possible.'

If our only fear is that we might fall short of becoming all that our Creator meant for us to be - 'a little lower than the angels' - then we must a find a way to overcome it through our actions in the world.

As Freemasons, we understand that our true centre is bounded by knowledge, wisdom, faith, hope and love and that, acting from that centre, we cannot err.

Knowing this, how can we be afraid?

Psalm 28

Unto thee will I cry, O LORD my rock; be not silent to me: lest, if thou be silent to me, I become like them that go down into the pit.
2 Hear the voice of my supplications, when I cry unto thee, when I lift up my hands toward thy holy oracle.
3 Draw me not away with the wicked, and with the workers of iniquity, which speak peace to their neighbours, but mischief is in their hearts.
4 Give them according to their deeds, and according to the wickedness of their endeavours: give them after the work of their hands; render to them their desert.
5 Because they regard not the works of the LORD, nor the operation of his hands, he shall destroy them, and not build them up.
6 Blessed be the LORD, because he hath heard the voice of my supplications.
7 The LORD is my strength and my shield; my heart trusted in him, and I am helped: therefore my heart greatly rejoiceth; and with my song will I praise him.
8 The LORD is their strength, and he is the saving strength of his anointed.
9 Save thy people, and bless thine inheritance: feed them also, and lift them up for ever.

Meditation 28

We should not underestimate the importance of our Masonic community. Although much of the progress we make in terms of our spiritual journey and many of the decisions we make about our direction are personal, we must acknowledge that the company of like-minded individuals is a great source of encouragement and support along the way.

We declare ourselves to be the brethren of all Freemasons across the globe. Beyond that, we aim to cultivate and live by our understanding that all people are our brothers and sisters. On another level we acknowledge that we have a particular affinity and closeness with the members of our own Lodge. These are the brethren whom we know and come to love and care about. They are the ones with whom we work in the Lodge, with whom we sit at our festive boards, with whom we become friends. And it is in those bonds of particular friendship that our brethren truly become a practical and real support to us in our aspiration to become the best that we can be. Their approbation means something to us; their praise makes us glad; but the possibility of letting them down or of acting in such a way that casts a shadow on the harmony of the Lodge - these are important and powerful tools and incentives to remain true to all of our obligations.

And so it is that, consciously and unconsciously, actively and passively, our Brothers prevent us from falling 'down into the pit.'

Psalm 29

Give unto the LORD, O ye mighty, give unto the LORD glory and strength.
2 Give unto the LORD the glory due unto his name; worship the LORD in the beauty of holiness.
3 The voice of the LORD is upon the waters: the God of glory thundereth: the LORD is upon many waters.
4 The voice of the LORD is powerful; the voice of the LORD is full of majesty.
5 The voice of the LORD breaketh the cedars; yea, the LORD breaketh the cedars of Lebanon.
6 He maketh them also to skip like a calf; Lebanon and Sirion like a young unicorn.
7 The voice of the LORD divideth the flames of fire.
8 The voice of the LORD shaketh the wilderness; the LORD shaketh the wilderness of Kadesh.
9 The voice of the LORD maketh the hinds to calve, and discovereth the forests: and in his temple doth every one speak of his glory.
10 The LORD sitteth upon the flood; yea, the LORD sitteth King for ever.
11 The LORD will give strength unto his people; the LORD will bless his people with peace.

Meditation 29

There is no doubt that to set our feet on a path such as Freemasonry - a path that leads, ultimately, to self knowledge and deeper spiritual understanding - is to set off on a path beset with challenge and difficulty. Given that the path is often so hard, it is natural to wonder why we would bother, but the truth is that, once we have understood that the path exists, we can never forget it. If we try to ignore it and go back to our state of not-knowing, we will not again find a sense of ease and inner peace because we will be trying to fool ourselves. We will be denying what we know to be true: that there is more to this life than material success and sensual pleasure.

When we act on what we know and take that first step, we do so knowing - because our ritual makes it clear - that there will be no material gain in this. If we tread this path, it is for other, higher reasons.

But the path brings its own rewards: we learn the value of brotherhood. We learn to trust in God and to find joy in our daily advancements; we come to understand, in fact, that lasting joy and true beauty are to be found in the holiness we seek.

Psalm 30

I will extol thee, O LORD; for thou hast lifted me up, and hast not made my foes to rejoice over me.
2 O LORD my God, I cried unto thee, and thou hast healed me.
3 O LORD, thou hast brought up my soul from the grave: thou hast kept me alive, that I should not go down to the pit.
4 Sing unto the LORD, O ye saints of his, and give thanks at the remembrance of his holiness.
5 For his anger endureth but a moment; in his favour is life: weeping may endure for a night, but joy cometh in the morning.
6 And in my prosperity I said, I shall never be moved.
7 LORD, by thy favour thou hast made my mountain to stand strong: thou didst hide thy face, and I was troubled.
8 I cried to thee, O LORD; and unto the LORD I made supplication.
9 What profit is there in my blood, when I go down to the pit? Shall the dust praise thee? shall it declare thy truth?
10 Hear, O LORD, and have mercy upon me: LORD, be thou my helper.
11 Thou hast turned for me my mourning into dancing: thou hast put off my sackcloth, and girded me with gladness;
12 To the end that my glory may sing praise to thee, and not

be silent. O LORD my God, I will give thanks unto thee for ever.

Meditation 30

Our aim, as Feemasons, is to make of our lives a place fit and worthy to be the dwelling place of the Most High; a temple and a monument to all that is good. It's not a solid building of bricks and mortar, of course, but a figurative structure, made of all that we say and do in every moment of our lives. It's made of our relationships with our family and friends; of our interactions with strangers; of how we treat those less fortunate than ourselves. It's made of the words we speak and the acts of kindness we perform. It's in our hopes and dreams; in our aspirations for a better life for ourselves and our connections and a better world for all. It's in our prayers and in our silences; in our thoughts and in our hearts.

We have all taken obligations to uphold the highest standards of behaviour and to see in every person a brother or sister. It is in the upholding of these obligations and in the commitment to do it a little better every day, that our daily lives become our acts of prayer, our expressions of gratitude and our songs of praise.

Psalm 31 (abridged)

In thee, O LORD, do I put my trust; let me never be ashamed: deliver me in thy righteousness.
2 Bow down thine ear to me; deliver me speedily: be thou my strong rock, for an house of defence to save me.
3 For thou art my rock and my fortress; therefore for thy name's sake lead me, and guide me.
7 I will be glad and rejoice in thy mercy: for thou hast considered my trouble; thou hast known my soul in adversities;
10 For my life is spent with grief, and my years with sighing: my strength faileth because of mine iniquity, and my bones are consumed.
14 But I trusted in thee, O LORD: I said, Thou art my God.
16 Make thy face to shine upon thy servant: save me for thy mercies' sake.
19 Oh how great is thy goodness, which thou hast laid up for them that fear thee; which thou hast wrought for them that trust in thee before the sons of men!
20 Thou shalt hide them in the secret of thy presence from the pride of man: thou shalt keep them secretly in a pavilion from the strife of tongues.
21 Blessed be the LORD: for he hath shewed me his marvellous kindness in a strong city.
24 Be of good courage, and he shall strengthen your heart, all ye that hope in the LORD.

Meditation 31

Freemasons do not shy away from the thought of death and neither are we strangers to the trials and tribulations of life. Like everyone who understands the fragility and transience of this earthly existence, we are constantly caught between two extremes of response to what we know to be true. On the one hand we have the absolute joy that can come from being truly 'in the moment;' of appreciating the beauty of the world; of feeling a profound sense of gratitude for our family, friends and connections. To love and be loved is a daily miracle and, if we cultivate the practice of remembrance, we enter into its 'secret pavilion.'

On the other hand, our lives are tinged with the sadness of loss and decay. We grow old and infirm; our loved ones pass away. We experience grief, frustration and anger at our sense of powerlessness before the relentless march of time. We are leaves, tossed on the wind, swept away on currents over which we have no control.

And yet we have before us the possibility of equilibrium; of finding a due medium between these extremes. From that calm centre, that point within the circle of our lives, we can appreciate the joy and acknowledge the sorrow but, at the same time, we hold firm to our rock and our refuge, knowing always that courage and strength of heart are available to us when we live out the tenets of our professed faith.

Psalm 32 (abridged)

Blessed is he whose transgression is forgiven, whose sin is covered.
2 Blessed is the man unto whom the LORD imputeth not iniquity, and in whose spirit there is no guile.
3 When I kept silence, my bones waxed old through my roaring all the day long.
5 I acknowledged my sin unto thee, and mine iniquity have I not hid. I said, I will confess my transgressions unto the LORD; and thou forgavest the iniquity of my sin. Selah.
6 For this shall every one that is godly pray unto thee in a time when thou mayest be found: surely in the floods of great waters they shall not come nigh unto him.
7 Thou art my hiding place; thou shalt preserve me from trouble; thou shalt compass me about with songs of deliverance. Selah.
8 I will instruct thee and teach thee in the way which thou shalt go: I will guide thee with mine eye.
9 Be ye not as the horse, or as the mule, which have no understanding: whose mouth must be held in with bit and bridle, lest they come near unto thee.
10 Many sorrows shall be to the wicked: but he that trusteth in the LORD, mercy shall compass him about.
11 Be glad in the LORD, and rejoice, ye righteous: and shout for joy, all ye that are upright in heart.

Meditation 32

It's a recurring theme, not only in Freemasonry, but also in many of the world's religions and spiritual disciplines: to be our best, to interact with our fellows in kindness and generosity of heart, we need to be free from the burden of guilt that can weigh us down and render us, as it were, unserviceable.

There are a few ways to live guilt-free. The first is to be completely amoral: to live without any consciousness of the concept of right and wrong; to be insensitive to another's needs or pain - in other words to live a life of ego-driven self-centredness. This isn't an option open to Freemasons because - happily - we are, by definition, people who care about others and who do have a sense of morality.

The second way to live guilt-free is to never do anything wrong. This isn't an option for Freemasons either by virtue of the simple fact that we are human and therefore imperfect.

The third way is to acknowledge our mistakes and to seek forgiveness and make restituion. This is the only practical way to wipe our slate clean and allow us to approach each day with the lightness and clarity that are the marks of a fully functioning, well-balanced personality.

To learn to trust in the power of forgiveness and to embrace the gift of self-reflection that makes us human: these are the first steps on the path that will lead us to that sense of ineffable joy that is our birthright.

Psalm 33 (abridged)

Rejoice in the LORD, O ye righteous: for praise is comely for the upright.
2 Praise the LORD with harp: sing unto him with the psaltery and an instrument of ten strings.
3 Sing unto him a new song; play skilfully with a loud noise.
4 For the word of the LORD is right; and all his works are done in truth.
6 By the word of the LORD were the heavens made; and all the host of them by the breath of his mouth.
9 For he spake, and it was done; he commanded, and it stood fast.
13 The LORD looketh from heaven; he beholdeth all the sons of men.
14 From the place of his habitation he looketh upon all the inhabitants of the earth.
15 He fashioneth their hearts alike; he considereth all their works.
18 Behold, the eye of the LORD is upon them that fear him, upon them that hope in his mercy;
19 To deliver their soul from death, and to keep them alive in famine.
20 Our soul waiteth for the LORD: he is our help and our shield.
21 For our heart shall rejoice in him, because we have trusted in his holy name.

22 Let thy mercy, O LORD, be upon us, according as we hope in thee.

Meditation 33

Music plays an important part in the ceremonies of religions and spiritual practices in almost every culture in the world. The power of harmonious sound, the unifying force of voices raised together in songs of praise: these are vital foundations in the superstructure that we hope to build in and of our lives.

As Freemasons, we have our own musical traditions: our opening and closing odes; the incidental music that permeates our ceremonies; the songs at the festive board: the Master's Song, the Entered Apprentice's song. In their singing, we find the simplest and most direct route to creating unity amongst ourselves as we, literally, create harmony easily and instantly.

As Freemasonry seeks to modernise itself and to become more relevant to our 21st century lives, it is important that we do not fall into the error of thinking that the music in our rituals and at our tables is an incidental 'extra' that can be dispensed with when time is short.

We Freemasons understand the power of the spoken word. We would do well to consider and reaffirm the equal - perhaps greater - power of music and song to unite us.

Psalm 34 (abridged)

I will bless the LORD at all times: his praise shall continually be in my mouth.
3 O magnify the LORD with me, and let us exalt his name together.
4 I sought the LORD, and he heard me, and delivered me from all my fears.
7 The angel of the LORD encampeth round about them that fear him, and delivereth them.
8 O taste and see that the LORD is good: blessed is the man that trusteth in him.
9 O fear the LORD, ye his saints: for there is no want to them that fear him.
12 What man is he that desireth life, and loveth many days, that he may see good?
13 Keep thy tongue from evil, and thy lips from speaking guile.
14 Depart from evil, and do good; seek peace, and pursue it.
15 The eyes of the LORD are upon the righteous, and his ears are open unto their cry.
17 The righteous cry, and the LORD heareth, and delivereth them out of all their troubles.
18 The LORD is nigh unto them that are of a broken heart; and saveth such as be of a contrite spirit.
19 Many are the afflictions of the righteous: but the LORD delivereth him out of them all.

20 He keepeth all his bones: not one of them is broken.
21 Evil shall slay the wicked: and they that hate the righteous shall be desolate.
22 The LORD redeemeth the soul of his servants: and none of them that trust in him shall be desolate.

Meditation 34

While we try our best to live good lives, to be upright and true, we acknowledge that we sometimes fall short. We know in our hearts what is right and, in our moments of strength and certainty, we act upon that knowledge without hesitation.

But we all have moments of weakness and doubt as well and it is at these times that the companionship and support of our brethren is so important. It can offer us what we need to move forward, to power through those dark moments of uncertainty when we lose our way and our faith falters or is submerged under the sea of troubles that threatens to overwhelm us.

This is what our Brotherhood is for: to help each other - as well as the stranger at the gate - to find our way again. It's why we come together to unite in forming a column of mutual aid and support, recognising that we are stronger together than apart. It's why we should never be reticent to ask for help, for how can we be afraid to ask for that which has already been freely promised?

Psalm 35 (abridged)

Plead my cause, O LORD, with them that strive with me: fight against them that fight against me.
5 Let them be as chaff before the wind: and let the angel of the LORD chase them.
9 And my soul shall be joyful in the LORD: it shall rejoice in his salvation.
10 All my bones shall say, LORD, who is like unto thee, which deliverest the poor from him that is too strong for him, yea, the poor and the needy from him that spoileth him?
18 I will give thee thanks in the great congregation: I will praise thee among much people.
19 Let not them that are mine enemies wrongfully rejoice over me: neither let them wink with the eye that hate me without a cause.
20 For they speak not peace: but they devise deceitful matters against them that are quiet in the land.
21 Yea, they opened their mouth wide against me, and said, Aha, aha, our eye hath seen it.
22 This thou hast seen, O LORD: keep not silence: O Lord, be not far from me.
23 Stir up thyself, and awake to my judgment, even unto my cause, my God and my Lord.
24 Judge me, O LORD my God, according to thy righteousness; and let them not rejoice over me.

27 Let them shout for joy, and be glad, that favour my righteous cause: yea, let them say continually, Let the LORD be magnified, which hath pleasure in the prosperity of his servant.
28 And my tongue shall speak of thy righteousness and of thy praise all the day long.

Meditation 35

A Freemason is always a friend to the poor, distressed and lonely. Much of what we do in the 'outside' world involves charitable giving to worthy causes and there is no doubt that all Freemasons, rich and poor, can feel proud of what our institutions do to help those less fortunate than ourselves.
Ideally, we should do more than give money if we can. While we might thank God for our good fortune, we should also cultivate the practice of seeing ourselves as the vehicles by which God manifests blessings to others. So, when we involve ourselves directly in people's lives, doing good work through actual human contact, we are not only representing Freemasonry but also everything that Freemasonry stands for in terms of its understanding of and belief in the brotherhood of humankind.
Charitable giving of money is a worthwhile and laudable pursuit; charitable giving of our time and energy is even better. Giving of ourselves in the spirit of brotherhood is best of all.
Let us each determine to give what we can, whenever we can.

Psalm 36

The transgression of the wicked saith within my heart, that there is no fear of God before his eyes.
2 For he flattereth himself in his own eyes, until his iniquity be found to be hateful.
3 The words of his mouth are iniquity and deceit: he hath left off to be wise, and to do good.
4 He deviseth mischief upon his bed; he setteth himself in a way that is not good; he abhorreth not evil.
5 Thy mercy, O LORD, is in the heavens; and thy faithfulness reacheth unto the clouds.
6 Thy righteousness is like the great mountains; thy judgments are a great deep: O LORD, thou preservest man and beast.
7 How excellent is thy lovingkindness, O God! therefore the children of men put their trust under the shadow of thy wings.
8 They shall be abundantly satisfied with the fatness of thy house; and thou shalt make them drink of the river of thy pleasures.
9 For with thee is the fountain of life: in thy light shall we see light.
10 O continue thy lovingkindness unto them that know thee; and thy righteousness to the upright in heart.
11 Let not the foot of pride come against me, and let not the hand of the wicked remove me.

12 There are the workers of iniquity fallen: they are cast down, and shall not be able to rise.

Meditation 36

We have to cope every day with people who do not share our views and, worse, those who consider Freemasonry to be a negative force in the world. Obviously, we will do our best to correct misconceptions and prejudices and we will always judge a person by their actions, not on their professed belief or lack thereof.

However, we are not here to proselytize and we know that arguing with people determined to hold on to their prejudices is a waste of time. We must learn to let go of such potential disturbances to our peace, such upsetters of our equilibrium, and be prepared to let our actions speak the truth that we act in the best interests of all - including, unashamedly, ourselves and our connections - and we do it from a firm and unshakeable centre of hope, of love and of faith.

Psalm 37 (abridged)

Fret not thyself because of evildoers, neither be thou envious against the workers of iniquity.
2 For they shall soon be cut down like the grass, and wither as the green herb.
3 Trust in the LORD, and do good; so shalt thou dwell in the land, and verily thou shalt be fed.
4 Delight thyself also in the LORD; and he shall give thee the desires of thine heart.
5 Commit thy way unto the LORD; trust also in him; and he shall bring it to pass.
6 And he shall bring forth thy righteousness as the light, and thy judgment as the noonday.
11 But the meek shall inherit the earth; and shall delight themselves in the abundance of peace.
23 The steps of a good man are ordered by the LORD: and he delighteth in his way.
24 Though he fall, he shall not be utterly cast down: for the LORD upholdeth him with his hand.
30 The mouth of the righteous speaketh wisdom, and his tongue talketh of judgment.
31 The law of his God is in his heart; none of his steps shall slide.
35 I have seen the wicked in great power, and spreading himself like a green bay tree.
36 Yet he passed away, and, lo, he was not: yea, I sought

him, but he could not be found.
37 Mark the perfect man, and behold the upright: for the end of that man is peace.

Meditation 37

Luckily for us, it's not our responsibility to put the world to rights. Our duty is to live good lives of honesty and integrity and to deal kindly and sympathetically with all those who come within our compass. Some of us have more influence in the world than others, it is true, but we are only called upon to do what we can - no more but, equally, no less.

The world will continue to unfold as it should or at least as it will and we will only find peace by allowing that to happen. Again, we will always try to be influences and examples for the good, but we trust in God for the outcome, knowing that, ultimately, power does not lie with us.

Thus we are left with a strong sense that we must work always for the good but, at the same time, we must not allow ourselves to be overwhelmed by concern about the results of our actions. We work with a benevolent disinterest and in that way we remain conscious of that power, greater than ours, by whose hand all things come to pass.

There is no doubt that this is the path to find peace in this troubled world; this is the perfect way.

Psalm 38 (abridged)

O LORD, rebuke me not in thy wrath: neither chasten me in thy hot displeasure.
2 For thine arrows stick fast in me, and thy hand presseth me sore.
3 There is no soundness in my flesh because of thine anger; neither is there any rest in my bones because of my sin.
9 Lord, all my desire is before thee; and my groaning is not hid from thee.
10 My heart panteth, my strength faileth me: as for the light of mine eyes, it also is gone from me.
11 My lovers and my friends stand aloof from my sore; and my kinsmen stand afar off.
12 They also that seek after my life lay snares for me: and they that seek my hurt speak mischievous things, and imagine deceits all the day long.
13 But I, as a deaf man, heard not; and I was as a dumb man that openeth not his mouth.
14 Thus I was as a man that heareth not, and in whose mouth are no reproofs.
15 For in thee, O LORD, do I hope: thou wilt hear, O Lord my God.
16 For I said, Hear me, lest otherwise they should rejoice over me: when my foot slippeth, they magnify themselves against me.
17 For I am ready to halt, and my sorrow is continually

before me.
18 For I will declare mine iniquity; I will be sorry for my sin.
21 Forsake me not, O LORD: O my God, be not far from me.
22 Make haste to help me, O Lord my salvation.

Meditation 38

Rooted in our faith, Freemasons are in a position to walk through this world untroubled by the extremes of emotion and suffering to which so many people fall prey.
It's not that we are unmoved by what we see - indeed Freemasons are often the first to respond to suffering and crisis and we are exemplary in our efforts to help those in need - it's more a case of us understanding that this life is not all that there is and that suffering and pain, as much as joy and well-being, are transitory and, therefore, unreal.
Our ritual tells us clearly that this life is a shadow - darkness visible - and that true life and true light are only to be found on the other side of that mysterious veil that divides this life and the next.
With this in mind, we are able to face this life; to feel joy and sorrow, pleasure and pain, hope and disappointment with a degree of equanimity because our hope and our belief is in a life beyond this mortal realm, beyond the grave into which we will all be lowered and from which we will all be raised.

Psalm 39 (abridged)

I said, I will take heed to my ways, that I sin not with my tongue: I will keep my mouth with a bridle, while the wicked is before me.
2 I was dumb with silence, I held my peace, even from good; and my sorrow was stirred.
3 My heart was hot within me, while I was musing the fire burned: then spake I with my tongue,
4 LORD, make me to know mine end, and the measure of my days, what it is; that I may know how frail I am.
5 Behold, thou hast made my days as an handbreadth; and mine age is as nothing before thee: verily every man at his best state is altogether vanity. Selah.
6 Surely every man walketh in a vain shew: surely they are disquieted in vain: he heapeth up riches, and knoweth not who shall gather them.
7 And now, Lord, what wait I for? my hope is in thee.
8 Deliver me from all my transgressions: make me not the reproach of the foolish.
9 I was dumb, I opened not my mouth; because thou didst it.
12 Hear my prayer, O LORD, and give ear unto my cry; hold not thy peace at my tears: for I am a stranger with thee, and a sojourner, as all my fathers were.
13 O spare me, that I may recover strength, before I go hence, and be no more.

Meditation 39

There is a clear suggestion at our initiation that one of the conditions of our acceptance into the order is that the 'tongue of good report' is heard in our favour. In other words, our reputation - what others say about us - must be positive. It makes sense, of course. Why would we admit a person of whom others spoke badly without making further inquiry into their character?

The point is that words are powerful and the words we speak affect others around us, often in ways that we cannot anticipate. Knowing this, we can choose to harness this power as a force for good to build people up; to reassure, to calm and to bring joy; or we can use them destructively to bring down, to shatter peace and harmony, to cause sorrow and distress.

Hopefully, Freemasons, being committed to act for the general good, will only use this power positively, but a careless word, spoken in haste or anger or without thought, can lead us to cause untold harm unwittingly.

We are told that we must learn to guard our tongues in order to preserve our secrets. More importantly, we must do so to avoid causing distress. If we can find nothing pleasant to say, it is better to say nothing, always remembering that silence is a virtue highly prized amongst us.

Psalm 40 (abridged)

I waited patiently for the LORD; and he inclined unto me, and heard my cry.
3 And he hath put a new song in my mouth, even praise unto our God: many shall see it, and fear, and shall trust in the LORD.
4 Blessed is that man that maketh the LORD his trust, and respecteth not the proud, nor such as turn aside to lies.
5 Many, O LORD my God, are thy wonderful works which thou hast done, and thy thoughts which are to us-ward: they cannot be reckoned up in order unto thee: if I would declare and speak of them, they are more than can be numbered.
8 I delight to do thy will, O my God: yea, thy law is within my heart.
9 I have preached righteousness in the great congregation: lo, I have not refrained my lips, O LORD, thou knowest.
10 I have not hid thy righteousness within my heart; I have declared thy faithfulness and thy salvation: I have not concealed thy lovingkindness and thy truth from the great congregation.
16 Let all those that seek thee rejoice and be glad in thee: let such as love thy salvation say continually, The LORD be magnified.
17 But I am poor and needy; yet the Lord thinketh upon me: thou art my help and my deliverer; O my God.

Meditation 40

Among the many lessons that Freemasonry can teach us are those that help us to see more clearly where true value lies. We have an interesting attitude to social position and to wealth, for example. We pride ourselves on the fact that any good-hearted person can become a Freemason. We take pride in the fact that our members come from all walks of life and that, in Freemasonry, no outer distinction of rank or station makes one brother better or more valued than another.

At the same time, we take an equal pride in the fact that our 'rulers' often come from what might be considered to be the highest ranks of society. Even our ritual states that, "... in every age monarchs themselves have been promoters of the art..." as if this somehow gives 'the art' extra validity. In fact, we might also consider it the other way round: royal or noble patronage does not increase Freemasonry's worth, instead it reflects well on those who patronise it and adds to their status, suggesting, as it does, that even they "...prize honour and virtue above the external advantages of rank and fortune."

So Freemasonry teaches us to be content with our place in the order of things but, most importantly, it reminds us that our value is not determined by our social status but by our words, our actions and our hearts.

Psalm 41 (abridged)

Blessed is he that considereth the poor: the LORD will deliver him in time of trouble.
2 The LORD will preserve him, and keep him alive; and he shall be blessed upon the earth: and thou wilt not deliver him unto the will of his enemies.
3 The LORD will strengthen him upon the bed of languishing: thou wilt make all his bed in his sickness.
4 I said, LORD, be merciful unto me: heal my soul; for I have sinned against thee.
10 But thou, O LORD, be merciful unto me, and raise me up, that I may requite them.
11 By this I know that thou favourest me, because mine enemy doth not triumph over me.
12 And as for me, thou upholdest me in mine integrity, and settest me before thy face for ever.
13 Blessed be the LORD God of Israel from everlasting, and to everlasting. Amen, and Amen.

Meditation 41

All of our fine words and our high ideals are of little use to us - or anybody else - if we only espouse them in times of happiness, health and prosperity. When things are going well, when we are comfortably housed and our children are educated and fed, when our health is good and our wallet is

full, it is easy to be grateful, easy to thank God, easy to say, in the strength of our youth, "We do not fear sickness or death. To a Freemason, only dishonour is intolerable."

We know, though, that fortune's wheel will turn and that while we may be healthy and prosperous one moment, in the next illness can strike, work can become impossible and money can become tight.

It is at times like this that our faith is truly tested. How will we react when illness strikes us or one of our loved ones? Faced with our own death - or that of a loved one - will we still hold firm to that rock we claim is our fortress and our strength?

The true answer is that we don't know. We don't fully know how we will respond to crisis until it happens but there is no doubt that - while we can - we should prepare ourselves for what is to come. And, as we know from our initiation, preparation is twofold: inner and outer.

Our inner preparation here is about a daily practice of introspection: meditation, contemplation, prayer or whatever works for us. Through this, we learn to rely on our faith by force of habit - like a musician whose fingers continue to fall in the right places even as he loses his place in his music. Our spiritual 'muscle memory' needs to be tuned antomatically to God.

Our outer preparation consists of living according to the precepts that Freemasonry teaches so that, when the time comes, we can face whatever life brings secure in the knowledge that we have lived well and done our best.

Psalm 42 (abridged)

As the hart panteth after the water brooks, so panteth my soul after thee, O God.
2 My soul thirsteth for God, for the living God: when shall I come and appear before God?
3 My tears have been my meat day and night, while they continually say unto me, Where is thy God?
4 When I remember these things, I pour out my soul in me: for I had gone with the multitude, I went with them to the house of God, with the voice of joy and praise, with a multitude that kept holyday.
5 Why art thou cast down, O my soul? and why art thou disquieted in me? hope thou in God: for I shall yet praise him for the help of his countenance.
6 O my God, my soul is cast down within me: therefore will I remember thee from the land of Jordan..
8 Yet the LORD will command his lovingkindness in the daytime, and in the night his song shall be with me, and my prayer unto the God of my life.
11 Why art thou cast down, O my soul? and why art thou disquieted within me? hope thou in God: for I shall yet praise him, who is the health of my countenance, and my God.

Meditation 42

We often hear people say, 'Be careful what you wish for' and it's become one of those expressions that we use without really thinking about what it might mean and without considering its deeper implications.

There is a thought that runs through several spiritual disciplines and even some religions that says that this world is built on desire; that we get what it is that we most long for. It's not an easy concept to understand because it's impossible to imagine that anybody would desire a life of degradation and suffering, yet we can see that many people have one. There are two ways to consider the idea. The first is to simply say that it isn't true; it makes no sense. The second is to consider whether it's possible that, while nobody would choose to suffer, it is conceivable that a soul might choose to take on a life of apparent suffering in order to learn something and, even, in order to teach something.

These are deep esoteric concepts that require deep contemplation but the simple fact remains that, if we eventually get what we desire - if there's even a tiny chance that that might be true - wouldn't it be a good idea to make sure that our desires are fixed on the spiritual and not on the carnal?

Psalm 43

Judge me, O God, and plead my cause against an ungodly nation: O deliver me from the deceitful and unjust man.
2 For thou art the God of my strength: why dost thou cast me off? why go I mourning because of the oppression of the enemy?
3 O send out thy light and thy truth: let them lead me; let them bring me unto thy holy hill, and to thy tabernacles.
4 Then will I go unto the altar of God, unto God my exceeding joy: yea, upon the harp will I praise thee, O God my God.
5 Why art thou cast down, O my soul? and why art thou disquieted within me? hope in God: for I shall yet praise him, who is the health of my countenance, and my God.

Meditation 43

Nearly all of the stories told in our rituals have a positive outcome but they also have a moment of negativity too; a moment of tension that gives the positive added weight and value.

At our initiation we are put into darkness before we can be brought to the light. As Fellowcrafts we hear of how Jephtha was expelled from his father's house before being promoted to being the Gileadites' chief Governor. To become Master Masons, we must be laid in the grave before we can be raised again. In the the Royal Arch we descend into darkness to discover the source of light; in the Mark degree, the keystone is thrown over amongst the rubble before it is found and recognised.

So it is with life. There are always moments of darkness, doubt and negativity but they are invariably matched and offset by moments of certainty and joy. Knowing this and understanding the truth about how quickly the wheel of fortune may turn, we must try to maintain equanimity and not be unduly swayed by any extreme of emotion. Most certainly, we can avoid the depths of despair because we have chosen to have in our lives an inexhaustible source of hope.

Psalm 44 (abridged)

We have heard with our ears, O God, our fathers have told us, what work thou didst in their days, in the times of old.
9 But thou hast cast off, and put us to shame; and goest not forth with our armies.
10 Thou makest us to turn back from the enemy: and they which hate us spoil for themselves.
11 Thou hast given us like sheep appointed for meat; and hast scattered us among the heathen.
13 Thou makest us a reproach to our neighbours, a scorn and a derision to them that are round about us.
14 Thou makest us a byword among the heathen, a shaking of the head among the people.
15 My confusion is continually before me, and the shame of my face hath covered me,
17 All this is come upon us; yet have we not forgotten thee, neither have we dealt falsely in thy covenant.
18 Our heart is not turned back, neither have our steps declined from thy way;
20 If we have forgotten the name of our God, or stretched out our hands to a strange god;
21 Shall not God search this out? for he knoweth the secrets of the heart.
22 Yea, for thy sake are we killed all the day long; we are counted as sheep for the slaughter.

23 Awake, why sleepest thou, O Lord? arise, cast us not off for ever.
24 Wherefore hidest thou thy face, and forgettest our affliction and our oppression?
25 For our soul is bowed down to the dust: our belly cleaveth unto the earth.
26 Arise for our help, and redeem us for thy mercies' sake.

Meditation 44

Sometimes we have to tread our path alone. Sometimes it feels as though all support has been withdrawn and we have to be willing to embrace uncertainty, to take our first few steps not knowing for sure whether we are even heading in the right direction.

Relying on others, we must be sure that we don't lose confidence in ourselves. Relying on God, we must be sure that we are willing to take responsibilty for our actions. When we are uncertain, we must trust in our own sense of what is right and follow our intuition.

If it is the right path, we will know; if it is wrong, at least we will learn something from it before we find the right way again. We must remember that if we have to tread it alone for a time, there is a reason for this. We are not abandoned - ever - but perhaps we are being given an important lesson about independence, free will and trust.

Psalm 45 (abridged)

My heart is inditing a good matter: I speak of the things which I have made touching the king: my tongue is the pen of a ready writer.
2 Thou art fairer than the children of men: grace is poured into thy lips: therefore God hath blessed thee for ever.
7 Thou lovest righteousness, and hatest wickedness: therefore God, thy God, hath anointed thee with the oil of gladness above thy fellows.
8 All thy garments smell of myrrh, and aloes, and cassia, out of the ivory palaces, whereby they have made thee glad.
9 Kings' daughters were among thy honourable women: upon thy right hand did stand the queen in gold of Ophir.
10 Hearken, O daughter, and consider, and incline thine ear; forget also thine own people, and thy father's house;
13 The king's daughter is all glorious within: her clothing is of wrought gold.
14 She shall be brought unto the king in raiment of needlework: the virgins her companions that follow her shall be brought unto thee.
15 With gladness and rejoicing shall they be brought: they shall enter into the king's palace.
17 I will make thy name to be remembered in all generations: therefore shall the people praise thee for ever and ever.

Meditation 45

Some days, the sun seems to shine a little brighter, the breezes blow a little warmer and life is sweet and precious. This just happens and often for no particular reason. Goodness and happiness sometimes come into our lives as quickly and mysteriously as worry and hardship and if we are not to be trapped on an emotional see-saw all of our days, we must consider how to find equanimity in the good times as well as the bad.

It would be easy to allow ourselves to be swept away on the euphoria that the good days bring but if we allow that, then we cannot help but be equally affected by the doldrums that come with the bad days. If we choose to be ruled by our transient emotions, we must understand that we are not always in control of which emotion will hold sway at any given moment. In fact, our daily practice - our daily commitment to seek more light - should eventually lead us to be able to feel the emotions that sweep through us without being swept away by them. It will lead us in time to find that still centre from which we cannot err: that point within the circle that is bounded by wisdom and truth. From this still centre we will find a different kind of happiness, one not dependent on the vagaries of transient emotion; one more solidly founded on the truth of who we are.

Psalm 46

God is our refuge and strength, a very present help in trouble.

Therefore will not we fear, though the earth be removed, and though the mountains be carried into the midst of the sea;

3 Though the waters thereof roar and be troubled, though the mountains shake with the swelling thereof. Selah.

4 There is a river, the streams whereof shall make glad the city of God, the holy place of the tabernacles of the most High.

5 God is in the midst of her; she shall not be moved: God shall help her, and that right early.

6 The heathen raged, the kingdoms were moved: he uttered his voice, the earth melted.

7 The LORD of hosts is with us; the God of Jacob is our refuge. Selah.

8 Come, behold the works of the LORD, what desolations he hath made in the earth.

9 He maketh wars to cease unto the end of the earth; he breaketh the bow, and cutteth the spear in sunder; he burneth the chariot in the fire.

10 Be still, and know that I am God: I will be exalted among the heathen, I will be exalted in the earth.

11 The LORD of hosts is with us; the God of Jacob is our refuge. Selah.

Meditation 46

There are no real certainties in this life. We can plan and prepare for our future, of course - in fact, we must - but we do so in the consciousness that anything can happen at any moment to render our plans and preparation as nought. Sudden illness, accident, financial instability, earthquake, hurricane - these are things over which we have no control and, although we are statistically unlikely to be affected, we know from experience that statistical probabilty does not necessarily shield us from calamity or misfortune.

It is in our response to these crises in our own lives that our faith is tested and it is in our response to such crises in the lives of others that our true values are seen.

Freemasons, generally, are optimists. We believe in a benevolent God and we trust that life proceeds as it should. We do what we can to make things better for ourselves and others because that is what we are obliged to do and as such we take responsibility for our own actions and our own happiness.

Ultimately, though, we acknowledge that we are powerless in the face of forces we can neither control nor fully understand and it is in this state of powerlessness that we willingly and happily say, 'Thy will be done."

Psalm 47

O clap your hands, all ye people; shout unto God with the voice of triumph.
2 For the LORD most high is terrible; he is a great King over all the earth.
3 He shall subdue the people under us, and the nations under our feet.
4 He shall choose our inheritance for us, the excellency of Jacob whom he loved. Selah.
5 God is gone up with a shout, the LORD with the sound of a trumpet.
6 Sing praises to God, sing praises: sing praises unto our King, sing praises.
7 For God is the King of all the earth: sing ye praises with understanding.
8 God reigneth over the heathen: God sitteth upon the throne of his holiness.
9 The princes of the people are gathered together, even the people of the God of Abraham: for the shields of the earth belong unto God: he is greatly exalted.

Meditation 47

Freemasons, certainly those under the jurisdiction of the Grand Lodge of England, are called upon to express a belief in a supreme being as a prerequisite to membership. We use the word 'faith' regularly and it appears in our ritual. But what exactly do we mean by it?

Generally, the word is used to mean a belief in God or a religious or spiritual practice, usually in the absence of proof. In the past, when society was more homogenous, churches were full and the intercession of priests between the people and God was the accepted norm, God was external, outside of ourselves; a distant being to be placated or worshipped or petitioned. In those days, faith was, perhaps, a belief held in the absence of proof.

In these times, the idea that God is not just 'out there' but also very much present in our heart and part of our deepest self is more acceptable. Fewer and fewer people go to church and the idea that only a qualified priest can interpret God's word or wishes for our lives seems a little antiquated.

The sense that God is with us and available to us directly through prayer and meditation, through appreciation and the cultivation of gratitude means that more and more people are able to experience the presence of God for themselves, with no need of an intermediary.

In the light of this, faith becomes not so much a belief without proof, and more of a remembrance; a mindfulness of knowing.

Psalm 48 (abridged)

Great is the LORD, and greatly to be praised in the city of our God, in the mountain of his holiness.
2 Beautiful for situation, the joy of the whole earth, is mount Zion, on the sides of the north, the city of the great King.
3 God is known in her palaces for a refuge.
4 For, lo, the kings were assembled, they passed by together.
5 They saw it, and so they marvelled; they were troubled, and hasted away.
6 Fear took hold upon them there, and pain, as of a woman in travail.
8 As we have heard, so have we seen in the city of the LORD of hosts, in the city of our God: God will establish it for ever. Selah.
9 We have thought of thy lovingkindness, O God, in the midst of thy temple.
10 According to thy name, O God, so is thy praise unto the ends of the earth: thy right hand is full of righteousness.
11 Let mount Zion rejoice, let the daughters of Judah be glad, because of thy judgments.
12 Walk about Zion, and go round about her:
13 Mark ye well her bulwarks, consider her palaces; that ye may tell it to the generation following.
14 For this God is our God for ever and ever: he will be our guide even unto death.

Meditation 48

We love to imagine the temple at Jerusalem and the beauty of the holy mount. As Masons we hold on to three distict images of it that are overlaid, one on the other, separated by time. We see Abraham building the altar on which he believes he will soon sacrifice his son, Isaac; we see David offering up his prayers for the well-being of his people and, finally, we see Solomon's temple in all its glory, a wonder to all who saw it.

We, too, have our part to play in this still-unfolding story. The temple at Jerusalem may be but a memory and a symbol, but the building of another temple continues to be the work of every Freemason. Not a temple of stone, of course, but an edifice made of a life well lived; of relationships well tended, of love and kindness; of charity, brotherhood and faith. We are only human but we aim for perfection and even if we don't come close, our heartfelt efforts in themselves become a wonder and an inspiration for all.

Psalm 49 (abridged)

Hear this, all ye people; give ear, all ye inhabitants of the world:
Both low and high, rich and poor, together.
3 My mouth shall speak of wisdom; and the meditation of my heart shall be of understanding.
4 I will incline mine ear to a parable: I will open my dark saying upon the harp.
5 Wherefore should I fear in the days of evil, when the iniquity of my heels shall compass me about?
6 They that trust in their wealth, and boast themselves in the multitude of their riches;
7 None of them can by any means redeem his brother, nor give to God a ransom for him:
9 That he should still live for ever, and not see corruption.
10 For he seeth that wise men die, likewise the fool and the brutish person perish, and leave their wealth to others.
14 Like sheep they are laid in the grave; death shall feed on them; and the upright shall have dominion over them in the morning; and their beauty shall consume in the grave from their dwelling.
15 But God will redeem my soul from the power of the grave: for he shall receive me. Selah.
16 Be not thou afraid when one is made rich, when the glory of his house is increased;
17 For when he dieth he shall carry nothing away: his glory

shall not descend after him.
18 Though while he lived he blessed his soul: and men will praise thee, when thou doest well to thyself.
19 He shall go to the generation of his fathers; they shall never see light.
20 Man that is in honour, and understandeth not, is like the beasts that perish.

Meditation 49

The faith that relies on belief without proof will always be susceptible to doubt. The faith that needs us simply to remember and act upon what we know - because we have experienced its truth for ourselves - is much firmer, much harder to shake, much more rooted in our experience of ourselves and the world.
It is not always easy to find the source of that knowledge, however. We have to cultivate it through our commitment to live our lives in a certain way: through contemplation, meditation and prayer; through the practice of charity and the understanding of brotherhood we develop the sensitivity to discover God within our hearts. And having found it, we must develop a conscious practice to remember it and to live by what we know.
It may not be easy but the reward is profoundly worth it: a life of certainty, lived without fear.

Psalm 50 (abridged)

The mighty God, even the LORD, hath spoken, and called the earth from the rising of the sun unto the going down thereof.
2 Out of Zion, the perfection of beauty, God hath shined.
3 Our God shall come, and shall not keep silence:
6 And the heavens shall declare his righteousness: for God is judge himself. Selah.
14 Offer unto God thanksgiving; and pay thy vows unto the most High:
15 And call upon me in the day of trouble: I will deliver thee, and thou shalt glorify me.
16 But unto the wicked God saith, What hast thou to do to declare my statutes, or that thou shouldest take my covenant in thy mouth?
20 Thou sittest and speakest against thy brother; thou slanderest thine own mother's son.
21 These things hast thou done, and I kept silence; thou thoughtest that I was altogether such an one as thyself: but I will reprove thee, and set them in order before thine eyes.
22 Now consider this, ye that forget God, lest I tear you in pieces, and there be none to deliver.
23 Whoso offereth praise glorifieth me: and to him that ordereth his conversation aright will I shew the salvation of God.

Meditation 50

It is said that for evil to prosper all that is required is for good people to do nothing. As Freemasons we are enjoined to refrain from political involvement and the reason is clear: politics is potentially divisive and we strive always for unity. But we are also committed to help the poor, to support the underdog, to ease the burden and suffering of our fellows. How can we do that without entering the political arena?
The truth is that Masonic philosophy in its purest sense is idealogically far above the purely political. Freemasonry sees to the heart of the matter and is moved by suffering and injustice wherever they are found. Of course we vote (those of us who live in democracies) for different political parties and that is absolutely our right and our duty as private citizens. As Freemasons, though, we see beyond the divisions of party politics and we look for practical ways to help those in need. The hungry need feeding, the homeless need shelter, the sick need treatment, the despairing need something to hope for. Young people need guidance, old people need support, those who have fallen need to be lifted up.
This is where Freemasonry fits: not in the combative field of party politics, but in the unifying application of practical charity.
We know that all are our brothers and sisters and when we see them suffering we are moved to help.
Charity - love in action. It's what we do.

Psalm 51 (abridged)

Have mercy upon me, O God, according to thy lovingkindness: according unto the multitude of thy tender mercies blot out my transgressions.
2 Wash me throughly from mine iniquity, and cleanse me from my sin.
3 For I acknowledge my transgressions: and my sin is ever before me.
4 Against thee, thee only, have I sinned, and done this evil in thy sight: that thou mightest be justified when thou speakest, and be clear when thou judgest.
6 Behold, thou desirest truth in the inward parts: and in the hidden part thou shalt make me to know wisdom.
8 Make me to hear joy and gladness;
9 Hide thy face from my sins, and blot out all mine iniquities.
10 Create in me a clean heart, O God; and renew a right spirit within me.
11 Cast me not away from thy presence; and take not thy holy spirit from me.
12 Restore unto me the joy of thy salvation; and uphold me with thy free spirit.
13 Then will I teach transgressors thy ways; and sinners shall be converted unto thee.
15 O Lord, open thou my lips; and my mouth shall shew forth thy praise.

16 For thou desirest not sacrifice; else would I give it: thou delightest not in burnt offering.
17 The sacrifices of God are a broken spirit: a broken and a contrite heart, O God, thou wilt not despise.

Meditation 51

To live in the fullness of what it means to be human is to shine forth as a clear vessel for the light of God. In our purest state we are embodiments of the divine, embodiments of the love that is the bedrock of creation and the highest virtue to which we can aspire.
The clear mirror of our heart that reflects this love throughout our lives slowly becomes dimmed by the accretion of dust and grime that all our little human weaknesses lay on it over time. Our 'sins' - the actions we perform that are not born out of love and unity and understanding - eventually cause the mirror to become dull and dark and we can no longer fulfill our function to manifest God on earth.
This is why it is so important to keep that mirror clean. Freemasons have a clear set of guidelines that, if followed, will not only keep our mirrors clear, but will also help to clean off what has accrued in the past. Kindness, brotherhood, charity, love; gratitude, forgiveness, empathy. These are the the cloths and the polish that will keep those mirrors clear; the tools that we can use to make sure that God's gifts of love and unity come to fruition.

Psalm 52

Why boastest thou thyself in mischief, O mighty man? the goodness of God endureth continually.
2 Thy tongue deviseth mischiefs; like a sharp razor, working deceitfully.
3 Thou lovest evil more than good; and lying rather than to speak righteousness. Selah.
4 Thou lovest all devouring words, O thou deceitful tongue.
5 God shall likewise destroy thee for ever, he shall take thee away, and pluck thee out of thy dwelling place, and root thee out of the land of the living. Selah.
6 The righteous also shall see, and fear, and shall laugh at him:
7 Lo, this is the man that made not God his strength; but trusted in the abundance of his riches, and strengthened himself in his wickedness.
8 But I am like a green olive tree in the house of God: I trust in the mercy of God for ever and ever.
9 I will praise thee for ever, because thou hast done it: and I will wait on thy name; for it is good before thy saints.

Meditation 52

It may sometimes appear that we don't gain much by being Freemasons. We don't gain social standing, we don't gain wealth - in fact quite the opposite! The outside world can be quite scornful in its attitudes to Masonry and there is no doubt that our membership costs us money, if not in dues, then in what we give voluntarily for charity.

Invisibly, however, it gives us everything that we need to be happy in this world: a moral code to live by, brothers to walk beside us, companionship and laughter and, most of all, the knowledge that, when our time comes to face that grand leveller of all human experience, we will do so with a clear conscience and a glad heart.

By filling our lives with generosity and kindness and by always speaking thoughtfully and truthfully, we qualify ourselves to enter God's house when our earthly work is done.

Psalm 53

The fool hath said in his heart, There is no God. Corrupt are they, and have done abominable iniquity: there is none that doeth good.
2 God looked down from heaven upon the children of men, to see if there were any that did understand, that did seek God.
3 Every one of them is gone back: they are altogether become filthy; there is none that doeth good, no, not one.
4 Have the workers of iniquity no knowledge? who eat up my people as they eat bread: they have not called upon God.
5 There were they in great fear, where no fear was: for God hath scattered the bones of him that encampeth against thee: thou hast put them to shame, because God hath despised them.
6 Oh that the salvation of Israel were come out of Zion! When God bringeth back the captivity of his people, Jacob shall rejoice, and Israel shall be glad.

Meditation 53

We see all around us every day the consequences of living in a Godless world. Murder, hatred, violence: these are commonplace. Everywhere we look there are signs of degradation and despair.

Without the belief in a common ancestry, we cannot see each other as kin and so it becomes possible to hate our fellows; to see them as 'other', as different from ourselves; a danger and a challenge.

But once we acknowledge a supreme being, whether that is God as our father or the Earth as our mother, we have to acknowledge each other as brothers and sisters. And once we have done that, where is the room for hatred? How can we murder our brother? Or rape our sister? How can we hate those with whom we share bonds of heart and soul and mind? We must remove the scales from our eyes and the falsehood from our heart that let us see any other human being as anything other than as an extension of ourselves.

Psalm 54

Save me, O God, by thy name, and judge me by thy strength.

Hear my prayer, O God; give ear to the words of my mouth.
3 For strangers are risen up against me, and oppressors seek after my soul: they have not set God before them. Selah.
4 Behold, God *is* mine helper: the Lord *is* with them that uphold my soul.
5 He shall reward evil unto mine enemies: cut them off in thy truth.
6 I will freely sacrifice unto thee: I will praise thy name, O LORD; for *it is* good.
7 For he hath delivered me out of all trouble: and mine eye hath seen *his desire* upon mine enemies.

Meditation 54

If we believe that God is absolute - truly omniscient, omnipresent and omnipotent - then it is not so difficult to understand the power that has always surrounded the mystery of the Holy Name. If God's presence, knowledge and power are in-dwelling in the whole of creation, then how much more are they present in God's name?

In Freemasonry, we come to speak of God by way of a series of descriptive epithets: The Great Architect; The Grand Geometrician; The Most High. In the Royal Arch a great and holy name is revealed to us, so powerful that we are enjoined not to speak it aloud and alone but, rather, it may only be spoken when three are gathered.

And yet we know that, across the world, God is known by different names - just as holy, just as powerful - and so we are led to the possibility that either all these names are sacred and powerful or none of them are. Either the idea that God's power resides in the name is a true one or it is not. For us as Masons to entertain the idea that only one name contains these attributes goes against our Masonic understanding that God is One.

And so, we come to understand that, wherever the name of God is invoked and whatever name is used, God will be there for us, to deliver us from our troubles.

Psalm 55 (abridged)

Give ear to my prayer, O God; and hide not thyself from my supplication.
2 Attend unto me, and hear me: I mourn in my complaint, and make a noise;
3 Because of the voice of the enemy, because of the oppression of the wicked: for they cast iniquity upon me, and in wrath they hate me.
4 My heart is sore pained within me: and the terrors of death are fallen upon me.
5 Fearfulness and trembling are come upon me, and horror hath overwhelmed me.
6 And I said, Oh that I had wings like a dove! for then would I fly away, and be at rest.
7 Lo, then would I wander far off, and remain in the wilderness. Selah.
8 I would hasten my escape from the windy storm and tempest.
12 For it was not an enemy that reproached me; then I could have borne it: neither was it he that hated me that did magnify himself against me; then I would have hid myself from him:
13 But it was thou, a man mine equal, my guide, and mine acquaintance.
14 We took sweet counsel together, and walked unto the house of God in company.

21 The words of his mouth were smoother than butter, but war was in his heart: his words were softer than oil, yet were they drawn swords.
22 Cast thy burden upon the LORD, and he shall sustain thee: he shall never suffer the righteous to be moved.

Meditation 55

How lucky we are to be part of a society of sworn brothers! How joyful it is to know that friendship, advice, help and support are always there for us when we need it! How good it is to know that that friendship is based on something deep and meaningful and lasting.
But what a responsibility it is too. We are not just lucky recipients of those blessings, we are also the source of it for others. As we might call upon them in our times of need, so must we be prepared for them to call upon us in theirs. Then we must be the outstretched hand, the listening ear, the open heart, the strong support.
Our commitment to our Brothers means that we must be willing to be steadfast and true, knowing full well how devastating it can be when someone on whom you rely lets you down. Always in Freemasonry, our own needs should act as reminders of the needs of others and incline our hearts to help them. Even better if we remember that the world is full of our brothers who are not Freemasons.

Psalm 56 (abridged)

Be merciful unto me, O God: for man would swallow me up; he fighting daily oppresseth me.
2 Mine enemies would daily swallow me up: for they be many that fight against me, O thou most High.
3 What time I am afraid, I will trust in thee.
4 In God I will praise his word, in God I have put my trust; I will not fear what flesh can do unto me.
6 They gather themselves together, they hide themselves, they mark my steps, when they wait for my soul.
7 Shall they escape by iniquity? in thine anger cast down the people, O God.
8 Thou tellest my wanderings: put thou my tears into thy bottle: are they not in thy book?
9 When I cry unto thee, then shall mine enemies turn back: this I know; for God is for me.
10 In God will I praise his word: in the LORD will I praise his word.
11 In God have I put my trust: I will not be afraid what man can do unto me.
12 Thy vows are upon me, O God: I will render praises unto thee.
13 For thou hast delivered my soul from death: wilt not thou deliver my feet from falling, that I may walk before God in the light of the living?

Meditation 56

As Masons we are comfortable with our faith and happy to join with others under the widest of umbrellas: that we believe in a supreme being. Freemasonry, although its tales and legends are rooted in the Bible, appeals to people of all faiths for the simple reason that it allows each individual to conceive of God in their own way, free from imposed dogma. This liberality allows us an ease with faith and an ease with each other because we can all rest secure in the knowledge that, deep down, beyond the superficialities that divide us, we hold fast to the same unshakeable ideal of brotherhood.

In good times we wear our faith lightly; so lightly, in fact, that we can forget it's there. Life flows so smoothly that we forget whose hand it is that directs it and we forget the debt of gratitude that is due.

When things go wrong, though - when we are faced with trouble and distress - that is when the value of faith shines through. When illness and the shadow of death come close - when fear threatens to unbalance us - that is when we most have need of trust. That is the time when we know that our trust in God is well founded.

Psalm 57 (abridged)

Be merciful unto me, O God, be merciful unto me: for my soul trusteth in thee: yea, in the shadow of thy wings will I make my refuge, until these calamities be overpast.
2 I will cry unto God most high; unto God that performeth all things for me.
3 He shall send from heaven, and save me from the reproach of him that would swallow me up. Selah. God shall send forth his mercy and his truth.
5 Be thou exalted, O God, above the heavens; let thy glory be above all the earth.
6 They have prepared a net for my steps; my soul is bowed down: they have digged a pit before me, into the midst whereof they are fallen themselves. Selah.
7 My heart is fixed, O God, my heart is fixed: I will sing and give praise.
8 Awake up, my glory; awake, psaltery and harp: I myself will awake early.
9 I will praise thee, O Lord, among the people: I will sing unto thee among the nations.
10 For thy mercy is great unto the heavens, and thy truth unto the clouds.
11 Be thou exalted, O God, above the heavens: let thy glory be above all the earth.

Meditation 57

We often say that charity is love in action - that we are moved to charity by the spontaneous outpouring of love that results from our appreciation of the true implication of the fact that we are all Brothers under God.

The same can be said of mercy: that it is a spontaneous outpouring of forgiveness arising from a realisation that we are all weak, that none of us is perfect; that we have all done things of which we are not proud.

Charity inclines our hearts to generosity; mercy teaches us forebearance and compassion to others. It teaches us patience, gentleness and encourages an empathetic understanding of the troubles of others.

As we know, generosity begets generosity; kindness begets kindness; mercy begets mercy.

If we wish to rest in the shelter of God's love and mercy, then we must be prepared to offer those same comforts to all those who ask for ours.

Psalm 58

Do ye indeed speak righteousness, O congregation? do ye judge uprightly, O ye sons of men?
2 Yea, in heart ye work wickedness; ye weigh the violence of your hands in the earth.
3 The wicked are estranged from the womb: they go astray as soon as they be born, speaking lies.
4 Their poison is like the poison of a serpent: they are like the deaf adder that stoppeth her ear;
5 Which will not hearken to the voice of charmers, charming never so wisely.
6 Break their teeth, O God, in their mouth: break out the great teeth of the young lions, O LORD.
7 Let them melt away as waters which run continually: when he bendeth his bow to shoot his arrows, let them be as cut in pieces.
8 As a snail which melteth, let every one of them pass away: like the untimely birth of a woman, that they may not see the sun.
9 Before your pots can feel the thorns, he shall take them away as with a whirlwind, both living, and in his wrath.
10 The righteous shall rejoice when he seeth the vengeance: he shall wash his feet in the blood of the wicked.
11 So that a man shall say, Verily there is a reward for the righteous: verily he is a God that judgeth in the earth.

Meditation 58

We all have dark thoughts; we all have a dark side: a side that wants to call down destruction on those who wrong us; a side that wants to lash out when we are hurt or threatened. Our primitive instincts are strong within us and, when we give them free reign, they thirst for vengeance and retribution.

Yet also within us is a divine spark; an essential part of the divinity that resides in all of life and this tiny drop of water in the ocean of life, this shard or splinter of light that shines in our depths, is what has the power to lift us beyond our base instincts into higher realms of mercy and compassion.

Freemasons are not beasts. We work to subdue our baser passions and, while we acknowledge that they exist, we use the tools that Freemasonry gives us to transform their energy into finer stuff.

Thus vengeance becomes mercy, judgement becomes forebearance, intolerance becomes understanding, antipathy becomes empathy.

This is the true work of a Freemason: to turn the lead of our basest selves into the gold of purest Spirit. This is the true aim and miracle of alchemy.

Psalm 59 (abridged)

Deliver me from mine enemies, O my God: defend me from them that rise up against me.
2 Deliver me from the workers of iniquity, and save me from bloody men.
3 For, lo, they lie in wait for my soul: the mighty are gathered against me; not for my transgression, nor for my sin, O LORD.
4 They run and prepare themselves without my fault: awake to help me, and behold.
10 The God of my mercy shall prevent me: God shall let me see my desire upon mine enemies.
11 Slay them not, lest my people forget: scatter them by thy power; and bring them down, O Lord our shield.
12 For the sin of their mouth and the words of their lips let them even be taken in their pride: and for cursing and lying which they speak.
13 Consume them in wrath, consume them, that they may not be: and let them know that God ruleth in Jacob unto the ends of the earth. Selah.
14 And at evening let them return; and let them make a noise like a dog, and go round about the city.
15 Let them wander up and down for meat, and grudge if they be not satisfied.
16 But I will sing of thy power; yea, I will sing aloud of thy mercy in the morning: for thou hast been my defence and

refuge in the day of my trouble.
17 Unto thee, O my strength, will I sing: for God is my defence, and the God of my mercy.

Meditation 59

While it is true that forgiveness is one the greatest gifts that we can bestow on our fellow creatures, and while it is the blessing of God we most desire and need to live a full, open life, we cannot deny that sometimes our thoughts are taken by baser wishes.
Ultimately, we understand that we have no control over what others do or what befalls them as a consequence. We exercise a certain amount of power in our own lives by the choices we make, but even then, nothing is certain.
Which is why, in the end, to pray for particular outcomes is not only vain but leaves us open to the disappointments of false expectation and the weakening of faith that can accompany it. Our greatest prayer, in every circumstance, is joyful, total surrender: 'Thy will be done."

Psalm 60

O God, thou hast cast us off, thou hast scattered us, thou hast been displeased; O turn thyself to us again.
2 Thou hast made the earth to tremble; thou hast broken it: heal the breaches thereof; for it shaketh.
3 Thou hast shewed thy people hard things: thou hast made us to drink the wine of astonishment.
4 Thou hast given a banner to them that fear thee, that it may be displayed because of the truth. Selah.
5 That thy beloved may be delivered; save with thy right hand, and hear me.
6 God hath spoken in his holiness; I will rejoice, I will divide Shechem, and mete out the valley of Succoth.
7 Gilead is mine, and Manasseh is mine; Ephraim also is the strength of mine head; Judah is my lawgiver;
8 Moab is my washpot; over Edom will I cast out my shoe: Philistia, triumph thou because of me.
9 Who will bring me into the strong city? who will lead me into Edom?
10 Wilt not thou, O God, which hadst cast us off? and thou, O God, which didst not go out with our armies?
11 Give us help from trouble: for vain is the help of man.
12 Through God we shall do valiantly: for he it is that shall tread down our enemies.

Meditation 60

In the second degree we hear the story of Jephtha and his brothers; of how Jephtha was cast out and then reinstated to high honour. In the preamble to the story itself, we are told of how God habitually subjected the people '...to the inroads and oppressions of neighbouring gentile nations...' as a punishment for abandoning the laws of their forefathers. When the people repented, however, God '...never failed to raise them up a champion and deliverer.'

There are many points of interest to the tale but one of them in particular tells us a great deal about human nature and about the nature of God.

We are told that the people 'repeatedly' forsook the laws of their forefathers and that God 'never failed' to redeem them

What we learn from this is that it wasn't a one-off; a momentary lapse in judgement by the people - it was habitual. In other words the story tells us that, as humans - even though we Freemasons like to think of ourselves as 'good' ones - we will fall down; we will fall short; we will keep going wrong. It's in our nature: we are not perfect.

But, happily, it is God's nature to forgive. However often we err, however far we stray from the right path, God is there to wash away the past and let us try again. We are creatures of dust, animated by God's breath and that divine spark within us is love, a love that is merciful, kind and patient.

Psalm 61

Hear my cry, O God; attend unto my prayer.
From the end of the earth will I cry unto thee, when my heart is overwhelmed: lead me to the rock that is higher than I.
3 For thou hast been a shelter for me, and a strong tower from the enemy.
4 I will abide in thy tabernacle for ever: I will trust in the covert of thy wings. Selah.
5 For thou, O God, hast heard my vows: thou hast given me the heritage of those that fear thy name.
6 Thou wilt prolong the king's life: and his years as many generations.
7 He shall abide before God for ever: O prepare mercy and truth, which may preserve him.
8 So will I sing praise unto thy name for ever, that I may daily perform my vows.

Meditation 61

The obligations of a Freemason are many and varied and they bind us for life to certain ways of being.

Although they are one of the main things that the outside world often finds most threatening about Freemasonry, in some ways they are the most reassuring as they commit us to a life of selflessness, kindness and support for others, Masons and non-Masons alike.

Of course, the most obviously exclusive obligation is the one that binds us not to reveal the secrets of Freemasonry but in these days of the internet when everything is freely available, we must reconsider exactly what we mean by our secrets.

A non-Mason could be in possession of the signs, words and tokens of a Mason and still not pass muster as a true member as they would also need to be familiar with the ways in which they are transmitted. And even if they did get those right, every step along the road of untruth and duplicity will take them further and further away from what are our most precious - if open - secrets.

The peaceful mind and the calm heart that come from an untroubled conscience, free from the taint of falsehood, lightened by the sharing of troubles with brothers, attuned to the divine and to the highest aspirations - these are Freemasonry's true secrets and they are available to all who are prepared to work for the common good.

Psalm 62 (abridged)

Truly my soul waiteth upon God: from him cometh my salvation.

2 He only is my rock and my salvation; he is my defence; I shall not be greatly moved.

5 My soul, wait thou only upon God; for my expectation is from him.

6 He only is my rock and my salvation: he is my defence; I shall not be moved.

7 In God is my salvation and my glory: the rock of my strength, and my refuge, is in God.

8 Trust in him at all times; ye people, pour out your heart before him: God is a refuge for us. Selah.

9 Surely men of low degree are vanity, and men of high degree are a lie: to be laid in the balance, they are altogether lighter than vanity.

10 Trust not in oppression, and become not vain in robbery: if riches increase, set not your heart upon them.

11 God hath spoken once; twice have I heard this; that power belongeth unto God.

12 Also unto thee, O Lord, belongeth mercy: for thou renderest to every man according to his work.

Meditation 62

Freemasonry, through the symbolism of the level, teaches equality and recognises that all people are both creatures of the dust and sparks of the divine. Within our earthly frame resides an immortal principle that knows no distinctions of rank or station and it is to this part of what makes us human that our philosophy points.

There are dangers in the Masonic system though. We are an initiatory order and we ascend clearly laid out steps on the path that leads us from base materiality to the realms of the divine. On the way we collect honours and titles and, if we are not careful, the outer signs of our advancement will halt our inner progress altogether, leaving us outwardly elevated but inwardly stunted, seduced by finery and far from the path we first set out to follow.

Our ritual tells us that we are all equal and that means that the newest Entered Apprentice is of no less value within our system than the Grand Master himself. What differentiates them is time, experience and the knowledge and wisdom to be gained on the path. But if the search for knowledge and wisdom is forgotten in the seeking after rank and station, then rank and station mean nothing.

Our ritual speaks of advancement through merit and merit is gained through study, contemplation and the everyday application of our Masonic values. If we are to move forward, we must be sure of our intention.

Psalm 63

O God, thou art my God; early will I seek thee: my soul thirsteth for thee, my flesh longeth for thee in a dry and thirsty land, where no water is;
2 To see thy power and thy glory, so as I have seen thee in the sanctuary.
3 Because thy lovingkindness is better than life, my lips shall praise thee.
4 Thus will I bless thee while I live: I will lift up my hands in thy name.
5 My soul shall be satisfied as with marrow and fatness; and my mouth shall praise thee with joyful lips:
6 When I remember thee upon my bed, and meditate on thee in the night watches.
7 Because thou hast been my help, therefore in the shadow of thy wings will I rejoice.
8 My soul followeth hard after thee: thy right hand upholdeth me.
9 But those that seek my soul, to destroy it, shall go into the lower parts of the earth.
10 They shall fall by the sword: they shall be a portion for foxes.
11 But the king shall rejoice in God; every one that sweareth by him shall glory: but the mouth of them that speak lies shall be stopped.

Meditation 63

We become Freemasons - hopefully - because we have arrived at a point in our lives when we realise that there is more to this earthly existence than the endless cycle of work-eat-sleep; more than working hard to earn a living to pay bills and mortgages and taxes. We come from all walks of life and there is no doubt that amongst us there are some who struggle to make ends meet while others are lucky enough to be able to enjoy all the sensual delights that material existence has to offer.

Eventually, though, even the most delightful of delights lose their savour and our soul awakens to the idea that satisfaction needs to be found in something deeper, more long-lasting, more real. For a while we may be able to ignore this growing yearning but, once awake, it's hard to go back to sleep - it's hard to 'unknow' what we understand more and more clearly to be the truth.

And so it is, with souls thirsting for God, we arrive at the door of the Lodge, ready to knock, ready to take that first step into the unknown, from darkness to light.

Psalm 64

Hear my voice, O God, in my prayer: preserve my life from fear of the enemy.
2 Hide me from the secret counsel of the wicked; from the insurrection of the workers of iniquity:
3 Who whet their tongue like a sword, and bend their bows to shoot their arrows, even bitter words:
4 That they may shoot in secret at the perfect: suddenly do they shoot at him, and fear not.
5 They encourage themselves in an evil matter: they commune of laying snares privily; they say, Who shall see them?
6 They search out iniquities; they accomplish a diligent search: both the inward thought of every one of them, and the heart, is deep.
7 But God shall shoot at them with an arrow; suddenly shall they be wounded.
8 So they shall make their own tongue to fall upon themselves: all that see them shall flee away.
9 And all men shall fear, and shall declare the work of God; for they shall wisely consider of his doing.
10 The righteous shall be glad in the LORD, and shall trust in him; and all the upright in heart shall glory.

Meditation 64

The three guiding principles of our order are Brotherly Love, Relief and Truth. Like all of the teachings of Freemasonry, the idea of truth is multi-faceted and many-layered,

First of all, we understand the basic truth of the existence of a supreme being; then we accept the truth of our brotherhood under that divinity. Truth is also an aspect of our obligations: we are enjoined and expected to be truthful in our dealings with others and to be true to ourselves.

What we cannot control are the words and deeds of others and when they are untruthful, whether from ignorance or malice, it can be hurtful and damaging.

Freemasonry has many detractors and there are those who would have us believe that the path we walk is an unholy one. We experience it differently and rest secure in our trust in God and in our own intuitions and understanding. We know that our truth is strong and robust; that it can withstand scrutiny and the attacks of its detractors. We know that it will not let us down in the final reckoning because, in the end, we know that it is real. We know that it is true.

Psalm 65

Praise waiteth for thee, O God, in Sion: and unto thee shall the vow be performed.
2 O thou that hearest prayer, unto thee shall all flesh come.
3 Iniquities prevail against me: as for our transgressions, thou shalt purge them away.
4 Blessed is the man whom thou choosest, and causest to approach unto thee, that he may dwell in thy courts: we shall be satisfied with the goodness of thy house, even of thy holy temple.
5 By terrible things in righteousness wilt thou answer us, O God of our salvation; who art the confidence of all the ends of the earth, and of them that are afar off upon the sea:
6 Which by his strength setteth fast the mountains; being girded with power:
7 Which stilleth the noise of the seas, the noise of their waves, and the tumult of the people.
8 They also that dwell in the uttermost parts are afraid at thy tokens: thou makest the outgoings of the morning and evening to rejoice.
9 Thou visitest the earth, and waterest it: thou greatly enrichest it with the river of God, which is full of water: thou preparest them corn, when thou hast so provided for it.
10 Thou waterest the ridges thereof abundantly: thou settlest the furrows thereof: thou makest it soft with

showers: thou blessest the springing thereof.
13 The pastures are clothed with flocks; the valleys also are covered over with corn; they shout for joy, they also sing.

Meditation 65

The seeking of truth and knowledge is one of the prime aims of a Freemason. Of course, we love the sense of fraternity and comfort that our meetings give us. Our social events and our festive boards are times of joy and laughter - and rightly so. It is '...good and pleasant ...when brethren dwell together in unity.' But we also know that there is more to Freemasonry than that. What goes on inside the Lodge is the key to what we are - and what goes on in the lodge is the unlocking of the secrets of who we are and what our purpose is here on earth.
Knowledge and understanding are good in themselves but we also hope that from them will spring the wisdom to appreciate that knowledge and to use it for the common good.
As Freemasons, our primary attitude is one of gratitude: for the beauty of the world, for our place in it and for the opportunities that we have to make it a little better and therefore a little more beautiful.
The knowledge and understanding that Freemasonry offers us means little if it does not lead us here.

Psalm 66 (abridged)

Make a joyful noise unto God, all ye lands:
Sing forth the honour of his name: make his praise glorious.
3 Say unto God, How terrible art thou in thy works! through the greatness of thy power shall thine enemies submit themselves unto thee.
4 All the earth shall worship thee, and shall sing unto thee; they shall sing to thy name. Selah.
8 O bless our God, ye people, and make the voice of his praise to be heard:
9 Which holdeth our soul in life, and suffereth not our feet to be moved.
10 For thou, O God, hast proved us: thou hast tried us, as silver is tried.
11 Thou broughtest us into the net; thou laidst affliction upon our loins.
12 Thou hast caused men to ride over our heads; we went through fire and through water: but thou broughtest us out into a wealthy place.
13 I will go into thy house with burnt offerings: I will pay thee my vows,
14 Which my lips have uttered, and my mouth hath spoken, when I was in trouble.
16 Come and hear, all ye that fear God, and I will declare what he hath done for my soul.

17 I cried unto him with my mouth, and he was extolled with my tongue.
19 But verily God hath heard me; he hath attended to the voice of my prayer.
20 Blessed be God, which hath not turned away my prayer, nor his mercy from me.

Meditation 66

We are told at the end of the lecture on the first degree tracing board that the distinguishing characteristics of a good Freemason are, '...virtue, honour and mercy.' These are fine attributes and there is no question that we should aspire to develop them in all aspects of our lives.

However, we might also like to consider a fourth 'distinguishing characteristic' which could be considered to be a natural by-product of the other three: happiness.

When we live our lives according to 'Masonic line and rule' we align ourselves with the true and lasting values that they represent; we follow the path we were meant to tread; we fulfill our proper role as co-creators of God's world. Knowing that all these things are true and also secure in our faith and the hope that it gives us, how can we be anything other than full of gratitude and joy?

Psalm 67

God be merciful unto us, and bless us; and cause his face to shine upon us; Selah.
2 That thy way may be known upon earth, thy saving health among all nations.
3 Let the people praise thee, O God; let all the people praise thee.
4 O let the nations be glad and sing for joy: for thou shalt judge the people righteously, and govern the nations upon earth. Selah.
5 Let the people praise thee, O God; let all the people praise thee.
6 Then shall the earth yield her increase; and God, even our own God, shall bless us.
7 God shall bless us; and all the ends of the earth shall fear him.

Meditation 67

There is no doubt that gratitude is the fertile soil in which contentment grows. To wake up every morning with a grateful heart is to take active, conscious measures to ensure our own well-being and happiness.

We have so much to be grateful for: we are alive on this beautiful world; we have the friendship and support of our brethren; we have our faith in God. Even in times of difficulty, when finances are difficult or when relationships go awry, to have these three things is to be in possession of great treasures because when worldy wealth is gone and the time of truth is at hand, it is love and gratitude that will see us through to that brighter world where the blessed Architect '...lives and reigns forever.'

Psalm 68 (abridged)

Let God arise, let his enemies be scattered: let them also that hate him flee before him.
2 As smoke is driven away, so drive them away: as wax melteth before the fire, so let the wicked perish at the presence of God.
3 But let the righteous be glad; let them rejoice before God: yea, let them exceedingly rejoice.
4 Sing unto God, sing praises to his name: extol him that rideth upon the heavens by his name JAH, and rejoice before him.
5 A father of the fatherless, and a judge of the widows, is God in his holy habitation.
29 Because of thy temple at Jerusalem shall kings bring presents unto thee.
31 Princes shall come out of Egypt; Ethiopia shall soon stretch out her hands unto God.
32 Sing unto God, ye kingdoms of the earth; O sing praises unto the Lord; Selah:
34 Ascribe ye strength unto God: his excellency is over Israel, and his strength is in the clouds.
35 O God, thou art terrible out of thy holy places: the God of Israel is he that giveth strength and power unto his people. Blessed be God.

Meditation 68

When our ritual talks about Freemasonry being universally spread over the surface of the globe, we should pause for a moment and consider the fact that this is not just a ritualistic formulation but also a statement of fact. We are able to number among our brethren people of every race and every religion: from every continent and every country. Our ritual is performed in many different languages with countless variations and local idiosyncracies.

It is one of the reasons why we should always encourage visiting between lodges, districts and even constitutions. It can be so easy to fall into the trap of thinking that the way our lodge does things is the only way and for the ritual that we are so familiar with to become stale and lose its power to stir us.

But in travelling and visiting, we come to understand that while the Freemasonry that we know and love can appear to be so different in its outer form, at its core it is the same;. In the same way we understand that God, whose names are slowly revealed to us as we progress, is known by many more names across the globe, but remains - always - the one true God.

Psalm 69 (abridged)

Save me, O God; for the waters are come in unto my soul. I sink in deep mire, where there is no standing: I am come into deep waters, where the floods overflow me.
3 I am weary of my crying: my throat is dried: mine eyes fail while I wait for my God.
8 I am become a stranger unto my brethren, and an alien unto my mother's children.
16 Hear me, O LORD; for thy lovingkindness is good: turn unto me according to the multitude of thy tender mercies.
17 And hide not thy face from thy servant; for I am in trouble: hear me speedily.
20 Reproach hath broken my heart; and I am full of heaviness: and I looked for some to take pity, but there was none; and for comforters, but I found none.
30 I will praise the name of God with a song, and will magnify him with thanksgiving.
31 This also shall please the LORD better than an ox or bullock that hath horns and hoofs.
32 The humble shall see this, and be glad: and your heart shall live that seek God.
33 For the LORD heareth the poor, and despiseth not his prisoners.
34 Let the heaven and earth praise him, the seas, and every thing that moveth therein.

Meditation 69

There is a tendency, when times are bad and things are difficult, for us to withdraw into ourselves. It seems to be a natural - if strange - instinct within us to not want to share bad news, even to feel ashamed of our difficulties and illnesses, - mental, physical and spiritual - as if they somehow are the result of some moral failing or insufficiency to which others are not prone.

Luckily, our brotherhood is so ordered that none of us should ever feel isolated for long. Within our lodges mechanisms exist to make sure that no Brother falls out of sight for long before someone - usually the Almoner or some close brother - will do what is necessary to check whether all is well. These mechanisms are real and practical supports for many brethren and those of us who take on those caring roles are to be praised and thanked and, of course, supported in their turn.

We live with the hope that our faith and our brotherhood will be enough to prevent us slipping into despondency, but life can be hard and we all have moments of despair. In those moments, it's good to know that we have help at hand, physical as well as spiritual.

Psalm 70

Make haste, O God, to deliver me; make haste to help me, O LORD.

2 Let them be ashamed and confounded that seek after my soul: let them be turned backward, and put to confusion, that desire my hurt.

3 Let them be turned back for a reward of their shame that say, Aha, aha.

4 Let all those that seek thee rejoice and be glad in thee: and let such as love thy salvation say continually, Let God be magnified.

5 But I am poor and needy: make haste unto me, O God: thou art my help and my deliverer; O LORD, make no tarrying.

Meditation 70

It's very strange that even when we go out of our way to show the world how positive a force for good Freemasonry can be, there are still those who denigrate us and who treat us with suspicion and anger.

It is tempting to respond with a touch of self-righteous indignation when this happens but we have to accept that some people are not open to new ideas and will only disblieve everything we tell them and twist our meaning to suit theirs. If we respond with the same negative emotions we only serve to reinforce their prejudices and build up even more resentment and lies.

In the end, we know that truth is stronger that untruth. It may be that lies are sometimes easier to believe and easier to spread but, ultimately, the truth is true because it is real. It is strong; it will be what lasts.

Pslam 71 (abridged)

In thee, O LORD, do I put my trust: let me never be put to confusion.
3 Be thou my strong habitation, whereunto I may continually resort: thou hast given commandment to save me; for thou art my rock and my fortress.
4 Deliver me, O my God, out of the hand of the wicked, out of the hand of the unrighteous and cruel man.
5 For thou art my hope, O Lord GOD: thou art my trust from my youth.
7 I am as a wonder unto many; but thou art my strong refuge.
8 Let my mouth be filled with thy praise and with thy honour all the day.
17 O God, thou hast taught me from my youth: and hitherto have I declared thy wondrous works.
18 Now also when I am old and grayheaded, O God, forsake me not; until I have shewed thy strength unto this generation, and thy power to every one that is to come.
20 Thou, which hast shewed me great and sore troubles, shalt quicken me again, and shalt bring me up again from the depths of the earth.
21 Thou shalt increase my greatness, and comfort me on every side.
22 I will also praise thee with the psaltery, even thy truth, O my God: unto thee will I sing with the harp, O thou Holy

One of Israel.
23 My lips shall greatly rejoice when I sing unto thee; and my soul, which thou hast redeemed.
24 My tongue also shall talk of thy righteousness all the day long:

Meditation 71

Truth wears many guises and there is never any suggestion that Freemasonry is anything other than one of the innumerable paths that lead to the refinement and spiritualisation of humanity and eventually to the feet of God. But that doesn't make the truths of Freemasonry any less true. All 'truths' are really just different framings of the one truth: that God is one and that we are all God's children. Everything beyond that exists to illustrate and cement this truth in our hearts and minds.
But because Freemasonry is true, it lasts; it stands the test of time. What was true in 1717 when the United Grand Lodge of England was formed, is still true now and will still be true in another three hundred years, even in another three thousand. We must remain confident in the teachings that Freemasonry offers. The moral code, the particular framing of truth that it carries - these are good and strong and timeless. We can live by them and teach them to our children without fear. They will not let us down.

Psalm 72 (abridged)

Give the king thy judgments, O God, and thy righteousness unto the king's son.
2 He shall judge thy people with righteousness, and thy poor with judgment.
4 He shall judge the poor of the people, he shall save the children of the needy, and shall break in pieces the oppressor.
5 They shall fear thee as long as the sun and moon endure, throughout all generations.
6 He shall come down like rain upon the mown grass: as showers that water the earth.
7 In his days shall the righteous flourish; and abundance of peace so long as the moon endureth.
8 He shall have dominion also from sea to sea, and from the river unto the ends of the earth.
9 They that dwell in the wilderness shall bow before him; and his enemies shall lick the dust.
12 For he shall deliver the needy when he crieth; the poor also, and him that hath no helper.
13 He shall spare the poor and needy, and shall save the souls of the needy.
17 His name shall endure for ever: his name shall be continued as long as the sun: and men shall be blessed in him: all nations shall call him blessed.
18 Blessed be the LORD God,

19 And blessed be his glorious name for ever: and let the whole earth be filled with his glory; Amen, and Amen.

Meditation 72

Solomon himself is the subject of this Psalm and, in a way, it contains a blueprint for the ideal ruler. When we finally come to sit in the Master's chair - the throne of Solomon - we would do well to consider the ruling of our Lodge in line with the attributes outlined here. Of course, justice, honour and mercy are familiar ideals to Freemasons but peace, too, is paramount. To bring peace and harmony to our Lodge is vital for its effective functioning and the Master's role is to embody and promote this peace as an example to all the brethren.

We know that being the Master of a particular lodge is not the highest office to which a Freemason can aspire and so it is also worth considering how we will act as we move yet higher towards Provincial and Grand Lodge honours and how our positions of increasing influence might be used for the good of Freemasonry and the world at large.

It is also good to consider the rulers of Freemasonry themselves. They carry a weight of resonsibility on their shoulders to guide the Craft safely into a strange new world. We pray that they, too, will be guided always by those truly Masonic virtues of truth, justice, honour and mercy. May they - with our help - bring peace and light to every dark corner their influence reaches.

Psalm 73 (abridged)

Truly God is good to Israel, even to such as are of a clean heart.

But as for me, my feet were almost gone; my steps had well nigh slipped.

3 For I was envious at the foolish, when I saw the prosperity of the wicked.

17 Until I went into the sanctuary of God; then understood I their end.

19 How are they brought into desolation, as in a moment! they are utterly consumed with terrors.

20 As a dream when one awaketh; so, O Lord, when thou awakest, thou shalt despise their image.

21 Thus my heart was grieved, and I was pricked in my reins.

22 So foolish was I, and ignorant: I was as a beast before thee.

23 Nevertheless I am continually with thee: thou hast holden me by my right hand.

25 Whom have I in heaven but thee? and there is none upon earth that I desire beside thee.

27 For, lo, they that are far from thee shall perish: thou hast destroyed all them that go a whoring from thee.

28 But it is good for me to draw near to God: I have put my trust in the Lord GOD, that I may declare all thy works.

Meditation 73

Every positive emotion has a dark shadow and, as we tread the path laid down before us, our constant struggle is to walk in the light of the positive and avoid the the shade it casts. Even love of God - surely the most positive emotion it is possible for a human being to attain - contains the seeds of danger for the unwary. When we first find love of God in our hearts, it is our particular conception of God that moves us and rightly so because the first part of our search is to find a way to understand and conceive of the Divine in terms that we can comprehend. It is only later, as our love grows more certain, that we come to understand the infinitely multi-faceted nature of the Deity and so come to realise that all facets show and reflect the Light equally.

In the early days of our faith, it is easy to look down on others who seem to have no conception of God at all; even worse, sometimes, is the tendency to take issue with those who conceive of God in a way different from ourselves. It is here that war and conflict arise and it is here that the great shadow stands, to cast darkness over all our spiritual progress.

We must hold fast to the Masonic virtues of tolerance and love if we are to pass through the darkness that this shadow threatens and come, at last, to the sunlight of the greater truth. There is no God but God and God is One.

Psalm 74 (abridged)

O God, why hast thou cast us off for ever? why doth thine anger smoke against the sheep of thy pasture?
2 Remember thy congregation, which thou hast purchased of old; the rod of thine inheritance, which thou hast redeemed; this mount Zion, wherein thou hast dwelt.
4 Thine enemies roar in the midst of thy congregations; they set up their ensigns for signs.
7 They have cast fire into thy sanctuary, they have defiled by casting down the dwelling place of thy name to the ground.
8 They said in their hearts, Let us destroy them together: they have burned up all the synagogues of God in the land.
9 We see not our signs: there is no more any prophet: neither is there among us any that knoweth how long.
10 O God, how long shall the adversary reproach? shall the enemy blaspheme thy name for ever?
12 For God is my King of old, working salvation in the midst of the earth.
21 O let not the oppressed return ashamed: let the poor and needy praise thy name.
22 Arise, O God, plead thine own cause: remember how the foolish man reproacheth thee daily.
23 Forget not the voice of thine enemies: the tumult of those that rise up against thee increaseth continually.

Meditation 74

Intolerance is the enemy of Freemasonry. Every form of prejudice and discrimination stands in direct opposition to the ideals and truths that we espouse. No religious dogma, no racial or cultural bias; no '-ism' of any kind has any place in any Lodge under any jurisdiction of Freemasons anywhere in the world.

More than this, Freemasonry must make itself the outspoken critic of discimination in all its forms and the greatest, most powerful tools that it has at its disposal are the words and actions of individual Masons.

It is up to us to be the the visible face of Freemasonry and to be ambassadors for its philosophy of inclusion and tolerance. This doesn't mean that we have to get embroiled in discussions about the pros and cons of identity politics - anything overtly political is beyond our remit - but it does mean that we treat every individual on his or her own merit and that we relate to everybody without prejudice, with open hearts and open minds, seeing in them nothing more or less than a brother - or a sister - of the dust.

Psalm 75

Unto thee, O God, do we give thanks, unto thee do we give thanks: for that thy name is near thy wondrous works declare.
2 When I shall receive the congregation I will judge uprightly.
3 The earth and all the inhabitants thereof are dissolved: I bear up the pillars of it. Selah.
4 I said unto the fools, Deal not foolishly: and to the wicked, Lift not up the horn:
5 Lift not up your horn on high: speak not with a stiff neck.
6 For promotion cometh neither from the east, nor from the west, nor from the south.
7 But God is the judge: he putteth down one, and setteth up another.
8 For in the hand of the LORD there is a cup, and the wine is red; it is full of mixture; and he poureth out of the same: but the dregs thereof, all the wicked of the earth shall wring them out, and drink them.
9 But I will declare for ever; I will sing praises to the God of Jacob.
10 All the horns of the wicked also will I cut off; but the horns of the righteous shall be exalted.

Meditation 75

By approaching all that we do in a spirit of service to the greater good and gratitude for our many blessings, we avoid the dangers that potentially threaten our spiritual growth.

Freemasons are committed to acting in this world in such a way that the idea of service should be second nature. We acknowledge the interconnectedness of all life and we know that the suffering of one is the suffering of all. In the light of this understanding, we do not become overly proud of our accomplishments and achievements; our fortune, our gifts and talents; our strength and our intelligence. Instead, we give thanks that we possess at least some of those attributes when we see that so many do not. We give thanks for our families and friends, our loved ones and our brethren, appreciating that we have what so many lack.

And then we put all those gifts to work in the service of that wider brotherhood we call life on Earth.

Psalm 76

In Judah is God known: his name is great in Israel.
In Salem also is his tabernacle, and his dwelling place in Zion.
3 There brake he the arrows of the bow, the shield, and the sword, and the battle. Selah.
4 Thou art more glorious and excellent than the mountains of prey.
5 The stouthearted are spoiled, they have slept their sleep: and none of the men of might have found their hands.
6 At thy rebuke, O God of Jacob, both the chariot and horse are cast into a dead sleep.
7 Thou, even thou, art to be feared: and who may stand in thy sight when once thou art angry?
8 Thou didst cause judgment to be heard from heaven; the earth feared, and was still,
9 When God arose to judgment, to save all the meek of the earth. Selah.
10 Surely the wrath of man shall praise thee: the remainder of wrath shalt thou restrain.
11 Vow, and pay unto the LORD your God: let all that be round about him bring presents unto him that ought to be feared.
12 He shall cut off the spirit of princes: he is terrible to the kings of the earth.

Meditation 76

There is a key Buddhist teaching that tells us that, in this world, things are not what they appear to be. It is an idea that is reflected in other traditions of course and Freemasonry is no exception.

We know that the outer values of the world are often different to the inner values that Freemasonry seeks to inculcate in those who choose to make it their path. We know the difference, for example, between worldy wealth and the true treasures of the spirit. We know that physical strength will fail in time while strength of character will grow stronger the more it is exercised, even into our old age; we know that power and influence can be snatched away on a whim; that the measures of worldly success are fickle and untrustworthy. And did we not learn unequivicably at our Raising that worldly possessions lead us directly to the cold grave from where only love can lift us?

Through the teachings contained in our rituals and, perhaps more importantly, through the company and support of our brethren, we are able to remember that truth lies behind and beyond all the outer shows of the world. We are able to hold fast to to what is real and what will last.

Psalm 77 (abridged)

I cried unto God with my voice, even unto God with my voice; and he gave ear unto me.
2 In the day of my trouble I sought the Lord: my sore ran in the night, and ceased not: my soul refused to be comforted.
3 I remembered God, and was troubled: I complained, and my spirit was overwhelmed. Selah.
4 Thou holdest mine eyes waking: I am so troubled that I cannot speak.
5 I have considered the days of old, the years of ancient times.
6 I call to remembrance my song in the night: I commune with mine own heart: and my spirit made diligent search.
7 Will the Lord cast off for ever? and will he be favourable no more?
8 Is his mercy clean gone for ever? doth his promise fail for evermore?
9 Hath God forgotten to be gracious? hath he in anger shut up his tender mercies? Selah.
10 And I said, This is my infirmity: but I will remember the years of the right hand of the most High.
11 I will remember the works of the LORD: surely I will remember thy wonders of old.
12 I will meditate also of all thy work, and talk of thy doings.
18 The voice of thy thunder was in the heaven: the

lightnings lightened the world: the earth trembled and shook.
19 Thy way is in the sea, and thy path in the great waters, and thy footsteps are not known.
20 Thou leddest thy people like a flock by the hand of Moses and Aaron.

Meditation 77

To those who have never experienced it, it's difficult to explain how dark the night can be when we are overcome with despair. Hopelessness; the sense that our lives are worthless and pointless; the feeling that we have accomplished nothing and done nothing right; the seeming impossibilty of finding our way back to the right path and of climbing back up to the light - at times like this it seems that we are alone and friendless, cut off by our own sense of desperation from those who love us (how unworthy of love we feel at these times!) Not even our faith can help us when we feel so far from God's mercy.
And yet...and yet...even here, in this isolation and darkness, help is there. God is unchanging; God's love is unwavering; God's mercy and forgiveness are boundless.
Be patient. Be silent.
Listen for that still, small voice.

Psalm 78 (abridged)

Give ear, O my people, to my law: incline your ears to the words of my mouth.
2 I will open my mouth in a parable: I will utter dark sayings of old:
3 Which we have heard and known, and our fathers have told us.
4 We will not hide them from their children, shewing to the generation to come the praises of the LORD, and his strength, and his wonderful works that he hath done.
7 That they might set their hope in God, and not forget the works of God, but keep his commandments:

Meditation 78

After these few introductory verses, this psalm is a long catalogue of troubles. Perhaps it was offered up as a warning of what happens if we stray from the paths we know to be the true ones, but there are other lessons here too.

The idea that younger generations can learn from the mistakes of their elders has long been the hope of many of us. It's so painful to watch our children make the mistakes we made to learn the lessons that we so painfully had to learn ourselves but it seems that there's no way of avoiding it. Instead, we can do two things.

First of all, we should not hide those dark and difficult lessons from our children: they will grow and be strengthened by their understanding. Our desire to protect and cushion them from life's problems can stunt them and weaken them - if we carry them everywhere, they will never develop the muscles required to walk themselves.

Secondly, we can show them, through the example of our lives, what it is to face the darkness without fear; what it is to be afraid but to move forward regardless. We can show them what vulnerability looks like and show them how it becomes strength. We can show them our faith and how it supports us.

Psalm 79 (abridged)

O God, the heathen are come into thine inheritance; thy holy temple have they defiled; they have laid Jerusalem on heaps.
4 We are become a reproach to our neighbours, a scorn and derision to them that are round about us.
5 How long, LORD? wilt thou be angry for ever? shall thy jealousy burn like fire?
6 Pour out thy wrath upon the heathen that have not known thee, and upon the kingdoms that have not called upon thy name.
7 For they have devoured Jacob, and laid waste his dwelling place.
8 O remember not against us former iniquities: let thy tender mercies speedily prevent us: for we are brought very low.
9 Help us, O God of our salvation, for the glory of thy name: and deliver us, and purge away our sins, for thy name's sake.
10 Wherefore should the heathen say, Where is their God?
11 Let the sighing of the prisoner come before thee; according to the greatness of thy power preserve thou those that are appointed to die;
13 So we thy people and sheep of thy pasture will give thee thanks for ever: we will shew forth thy praise to all generations.

Meditation 79

Everything we do, in the final reckoning, is a choice. We can look to our childhoods and say, "This is why I am like this," or "This is why I behave in this way," but, once we become adults, we have to take responsibility for own actions and not look to attribute them to outside influences - however real and powerful those influences might have once been.

It is the same with our feelings. We can either go through life at the mercy of the effect that others' words and actions have on us, or we can choose to take responsibility for how we react to others and for how we feel. It's so easy nowadays to be offended by someone else's words or actions, so easy to be upset or hurt or disappointed by what they say and do, but we must learn to understand that any power another person has to upset us or make us feel bad is a power that we choose - consciously or unconsciously - to give them and the decision to be offended or hurt rests solely with us, not with them.

We do not have power over others but we do have power over our own actions, thoughts and feelings and, of course, we have a great help and support in our Masonry.

Psalm 80 (abridged)

Give ear, O Shepherd of Israel, thou that leadest Joseph like a flock; thou that dwellest between the cherubims, shine forth.

3 Turn us again, O God, and cause thy face to shine; and we shall be saved.

4 O LORD God of hosts, how long wilt thou be angry against the prayer of thy people?

8 Thou hast brought a vine out of Egypt: thou hast cast out the heathen, and planted it.

9 Thou preparedst room before it, and didst cause it to take deep root, and it filled the land.

10 The hills were covered with the shadow of it, and the boughs thereof were like the goodly cedars.

11 She sent out her boughs unto the sea, and her branches unto the river.

12 Why hast thou then broken down her hedges, so that all they which pass by the way do pluck her?

13 The boar out of the wood doth waste it, and the wild beast of the field doth devour it.

14 Return, we beseech thee, O God of hosts: look down from heaven, and behold, and visit this vine;

15 And the vineyard which thy right hand hath planted, and the branch that thou madest strong for thyself.

16 It is burned with fire, it is cut down: they perish at the rebuke of thy countenance.

17 Let thy hand be upon the man of thy right hand, upon the son of man whom thou madest strong for thyself.
18 So will not we go back from thee: quicken us, and we will call upon thy name.
19 Turn us again, O LORD God of hosts, cause thy face to shine; and we shall be saved.

Meditation 80

When it feels as if all the sweetness and joy have gone out of life and the world loses its beauty and charm, we must know that the world has not changed - it is we who have lost sight of the things that are important to us.
It's easy to wallow in a sense of anandonment and separation but one of the key lessons of Freemasonry is that we are the determiners of our own destiny. We choose how we relate to the world and we choose Freemasonry as one of the filters through which we look at it. When that filter fails us - or rather when our strength to use that filter fails - it is not always easy to bring ourselves back to our usual poise of equilibrium and wellness and once more see the world as it is.
In these hard times we must look inward to find the bedrock of our faith and that still, small voice within us that never falters, that never loses its way and that will never let us down.
If we can find the time and the space and the inclination to be still and listen, that voice will be there to save us.

Psalm 81 (abridged)

Sing aloud unto God our strength: make a joyful noise unto the God of Jacob.
2 Take a psalm, and bring hither the timbrel, the pleasant harp with the psaltery.
3 Blow up the trumpet in the new moon, in the time appointed, on our solemn feast day.
7 Thou calledst in trouble, and I delivered thee; I answered thee in the secret place of thunder: I proved thee at the waters of Meribah. Selah.
8 Hear, O my people, and I will testify unto thee: O Israel, if thou wilt hearken unto me;
9 There shall no strange god be in thee; neither shalt thou worship any strange god.
10 I am the LORD thy God, which brought thee out of the land of Egypt: open thy mouth wide, and I will fill it.
11 But my people would not hearken to my voice; and Israel would none of me.
12 So I gave them up unto their own hearts' lust: and they walked in their own counsels.
13 Oh that my people had hearkened unto me, and Israel had walked in my ways!
14 I should soon have subdued their enemies, and turned my hand against their adversaries.
15 The haters of the LORD should have submitted themselves unto him: but their time should have endured

for ever.
16 He should have fed them also with the finest of the wheat: and with honey out of the rock should I have satisfied thee.

Meditation 81

However much we want to rely on an idea of God 'out there' somewhere in the vastness of the heavens, until we understand the truth that God resides always and most closely in the recesses of our hearts, we will never fully understand the true nature of our Creator.
In Freemasonry we hear of that 'immortal principle' which animates us and, although it is pretty obvious that we cannot all carry the entirety of what God is within ourselves, we do all carry a divine spark that is, qualitively at least, one with God. Just as a drop of the ocean has the same qualities as the ocean but is not the whole ocean; just as the spark of a fire has all the attributes of the fire but is not the whole fire; so we carry within ourselves a divine and immortal principle that is of God but is not wholly God.
If we look inwards; if we listen to our hearts and learn to hear that voice within, we will come to recognise and understand that divine essence within us and, through that daily practice, through that daily advancement, we will come, in the end, to know God.

Psalm 82

God standeth in the congregation of the mighty; he judgeth among the gods.

2 How long will ye judge unjustly, and accept the persons of the wicked? Selah.

3 Defend the poor and fatherless: do justice to the afflicted and needy.

4 Deliver the poor and needy: rid them out of the hand of the wicked.

5 They know not, neither will they understand; they walk on in darkness: all the foundations of the earth are out of course.

6 I have said, Ye are gods; and all of you are children of the most High.

7 But ye shall die like men, and fall like one of the princes.

8 Arise, O God, judge the earth: for thou shalt inherit all nations.

Meditation 82

Mankind has always looked to God to bring justice to 'the righteous' and to visit retribution on 'the wicked' and this invocation to God to "...defend the poor and fatherless, do justice to the afflicted and needy. Deliver the poor..." is both timeless and, to our shame, as necessary in today's society as it clearly was at the time of King David.

As Freemasons, our duty is clear. We act in the world and our aim is to do God's work, which we interpret as working for the common good, attempting to relieve the suffering of the poor and needy. In other words, when reading an invocation such as this, a cry for help, we treat it as if it is directed at us because we choose to see ourselves as hearing with God's ears, seeing with God's eyes and acting with God's love.

We do not concern ourselves with visiting justice on 'the wicked' because that is beyond our remit and our understanding. That, we will leave to God.

But to offer succour - yes. Definitely. That's why we're here.

Psalm 83 (abridged)

Keep not thou silence, O God: hold not thy peace, and be not still, O God.

2 For, lo, thine enemies make a tumult: and they that hate thee have lifted up the head.

3 They have taken crafty counsel against thy people, and consulted against thy hidden ones.

13 O my God, make them like a wheel; as the stubble before the wind.

14 As the fire burneth a wood, and as the flame setteth the mountains on fire;

15 So persecute them with thy tempest, and make them afraid with thy storm.

16 Fill their faces with shame; that they may seek thy name, O LORD.

17 Let them be confounded and troubled for ever; yea, let them be put to shame, and perish:

18 That men may know that thou, whose name alone is JEHOVAH, art the most high over all the earth.

Meditation 83

We live in tumultuous times. The winds of change buffet us night and day and we are battered constantly by conflicting world views, by dystopian, end-of-the world horror stories; tales of war and violence; imagined and real threats to our security and well-being; shootings, murder; natural disasters; nuclear meltdowns: everywhere we look, we can - if we choose - find a narrative of negativity that makes the world seem such an ugly, bleak and hopeless place.

Yet, if we lift our eyes, we can still find beauty; we can still find peace; we can still find love and brotherhood and unity. All the ingredients for a successful, peaceful and happy world are at our fingertips and it is only a lack of purpose, intention and clarity of thought that prevents us from grasping it and making it a reality.

Our job as Freemasons is to help build God's temple here on earth and we cannot do that if we choose to place our energies with those who preach doom and gloom. In spite of everything that is wrong with the world, we must remain positive and, step by step, brick by brick, build that edifice of love, peace and unity that will be fit to house the presence of the true and living God Most High.

Also available by the same author:

'Level Steps:
100 Meditations for Freemasons.'

'Hidden Depths:
100 Meditations for Royal Arch Freemasons.'